For you,
from Feli,
Canadian lit.
5/88

stories by

SCARS

w.p. kinsella

"Mr. Whitey" has appeared in *Windsor Review*, "Bones" in *Story Quarterly*, "Canadian Culture" in *Martlet* and *The Story So Far*, "Dreams" in *Pequod*, "John Cat" in *Tamarack*, "The Kidnapper" in *Plum*, "The Rattlesnake Express" in *This*, "Manitou Motors" in *Martlet*, "The Forest" in *Waves*, "Black Wampum" in *Descant*, "Fawn" in *NeWest ReView* and "Scars" in *Shadows*.

ISBN 0 88750 285 7 (hardcover)
ISBN 0 88750 286 5 (softcover)

Design: Michael Macklem

Printed in Canada

PUBLISHED IN CANADA BY OBERON PRESS

For Ann, who sings to me

mr. whitey

For Bev Morrison

If it hadn't been that Mr. Whitey Bremner was one of those kind of men who don't figure that Indians is people, things might have been a lot different for him, and for Judy Powderface and her son, Little Emmanuel.

Lots of white men don't figure that Indians is people but usually they never get in a position where they can do nobody any harm because of the way they think. I remember one time me and Frank Fence-post and a few other guys was cutting brush for a farmer up near Wetaskiwin when a thunder storm come up. The farmer, his son and his white hired man headed for the barn.

"What about them?" the son say to the father as they walking away.

5

"They're used to being outside," the father said. "They'll be okay."

I heard in town that Mr. Bremner be looking for a hired man. When I come up to his place I can hear a gun shooting. I come round the corner of the house and Mr. Whitey Bremner be sit on a kitchen chair on his porch and shoot his .22 gun into a gopher hole in a big pile of dirt just outside his back door.

Mr. Whitey got hair the colour of barley been all summer in the sun, and it be about as thin. He got a round red face that sweat most of the time, and small pale blue eyes. His body be pretty big around the middle. He wear overalls and Stanfield's Underwear with the buttons open to his waist. He got a box of .22 shells on the porch rail and he keep reload his single shotgun with his stubby fingers. He look up and see me and grin kind of a silly grin.

"My name's Silas," I say, "I hear you looking for a hired man?"

"Need somebody to help with the chores and the haying," and he laugh kind of an inbreathing laugh, though I don't see nothing to laugh about.

"I can do that."

"If you don't steal nothing you can sleep and eat in the house." He do that funny laugh again and go back to shoot at the gopher hole.

I hate farm work but I need the money. I been taking that course on how to fix tractors and stuff, but when summer come all I can ever get for a job is farm work or something else useless like that. I figure big companies, as soon as they see my name, Silas Ermineskin, probably throw away my application. Big companies don't figure Indians is people either.

I start the next day work for Mr. Whitey. He live alone in a big old house. Used to be that his mother lived there but she died four or five years before. I never been in too many white people's houses but this is sure a funny one. Lots of white people figure that Indians is dirty, but I never seen many houses dirtier than Mr. Whitey's. The house had

6

been built quite a long time ago by his parents, it was white frame but ain't been painted for a whole lot of years. It got a verandah on three sides. Right after his mother died Mr. Whitey had the house raised up to put in a basement, then he stopped work on it and left everything. You step right out on a whole lot of hills of dirt that been what was dug out from under the house. There is the gopher hole in them hills, some pig weed and that's all. You just figure how much of that gets tracked in the house when it rains and then double it and you got about how much dirt there is inside. Mr. Whitey like to fry up bacon and chops and the whole house be kind of greasy and waxy like the inside of a barn get in the wintertime when it be full of cattle.

I guess if Mr. Whitey don't care about the dirt there ain't no reason that I should. After supper he sits on the porch and shoots at the gopher hole.

"You ever seen the gopher, Mr. Bremner?" I ask him.

"Once or twice."

"Why don't you just hide and outwait him?" Mr. Whitey do his funny inbreathing laugh and just fire a couple more bullets into the gopher hole.

Mr. Whitey don't have much to say, but he feed me good and the first pay day he give me an extra ten dollars. When I thank him he say, "Most guys would have stolen twenty dollars worth of tools by now. You're a good Indian, Silas."

"I ain't dead," I say. He does his inbreathing laugh again but I don't think he catch on to the joke.

I kind of start to clean up the kitchen one time but Mr. Whitey say to me, "That's woman's work." Which is what I been hoping he'll say.

"Then maybe you should get a woman around here," I say real fast. "I know a good lady, she's real clean and she work hard, first couple of months just for room and board for her and her little boy, if you can't afford to pay her."

"What's her name?"

"Judy Powderface."

"How old is she?"

"27, 28, I don't know for sure."

"Sure wish my mother was still here."

"She don't steal either."

"Tell her to come around."

Judy Powderface been having herself a run of bad luck. First her husband Matthew got killed by a car while he walk along the highway one night. Then her cabin burn up while she was down to Hobbema one afternoon. She and her boy, Emmanuel, who be about six, live in with her uncle, but he got a whole houseful of kids already and sure be glad if she find someplace to go.

Judy Powderface be tall and slim with hair black and shiny as a grizzly bear that she wear in bangs on her forehead and braids on her shoulder. Her skin be kind of copper-coloured and her eyes flash in her face like water in the bottom of a tea kettle. She dress neat the day she come around, with clean jeans and a sweater the colour of wild roses.

Everything I tell Mr. Whitey about Judy Powderface is true, but what I don't bother to tell him is about Little Emmanuel who be what our medicine lady is call a shaman child. That mean he got a special way with animals, and Mad Etta say to me one time that she pretty sure he got the makings of a medicine man and that she sure gonna keep her eye on him.

Kids don't come much better than Emmanuel. He never run around and scream. He be pretty small for his age, got light brown skin, but his eyes be almost black and big and round as the bottoms of beer bottles. Emmanuel's head always seem too big for his body but I don't think it really is, it just that his eyes be so large.

Eathen Firstrider drive Judy and Emmanuel down one Saturday morning. They got all their stuff in a couple of cardboard boxes there in the back of Blind Louis Coyote's pickup. I can see Judy's face kind of drop when she first get a look at the inside of the house but she just kind of set her back and ask where the cleaning stuff is. Mr. Whitey is kind of step around the kitchen like maybe he is in the way and he tell Judy to make up a list and he'll go to town for it

8

right away. Little Emmanuel never say nothing to nobody, he just play around on the piles of dirt outside the door.

After supper Judy is stand at the screen door and watch Mr. Whitey shoot into the gopher hole.

"If you kill it don't expect me to cook it up," Judy say, and make kind of a shy laugh.

Mr. Whitey don't act like he know if she joking or not, he just smile real wide and do his inbreathing laugh.

It don't take long before Judy Powderface is make that farm kind of a nice place to live. She cook up good meals and she scrub and clean. One day she ask Mr. Whitey for paint and he stop work right in the middle of the day to go to town and get it. Judy make the kitchen yellow with light blue trim, and she shine up the windows and put up a curtain that she found in a drawer someplace. She got me to put down some planks outside the back door so we don't track dirt and mud into the house no more.

In the evenings we sit around and drink tea and listen to the Camrose radio station that plays country music. Mr. Whitey tap his foot along with the music and say that someplace he got a fiddle put away and maybe he get it out one day and play for us. He talk about getting the electricity installed in the house and maybe finishing up the basement.

Mr. Whitey never mention it but I hear from somebody in town that he went for a lot of years with one of the Hurtubise girls from over by Bittern Lake, and how they figured on get married except he had his old mother to look after. After his mother died he started to fix the place up but that Hurtubise girl is change her mind about marrying him and that's when he start to let the place go pretty bad, at least that's what some folks in town say.

I never seen Emmanuel talk to anyone but Judy and then not much. I guess Judy explain to him that Mr. Whitey want to get that gopher out of the hole in the ground and that be why he shoot at it the way he does.

One morning I get up about 6.30 and there is Emmanuel sit in front of the gopher hole on crossed legs with a handful of greens held out toward the hole. When I come in for lunch he still be sitting there and at 5.30 he still be right where he was in the morning. After supper Judy is just pick him up and put him to bed or I suppose he would of stayed there all night. Mr. Whitey don't shoot in the gopher hole that night. We just sit on the porch and listen to the radio and he keep saying, "I never seen nothin like that little boy," and he scratch his big yellow head and laugh.

In the morning Emmanuel be right back like he was the day before. On the third day at supper Judy say that that afternoon the gopher come out and ate some of the greens from Emmanuel's hand, but it be about three days more before we get to see it. After supper one night Judy call us to the window and there is the gopher about half way out of his hole be nibble on the stuff Little Emmanuel hold out for him. Mr. Whitey do his inbreathing laugh.

After that the gopher he come out regular to eat Emmanuel's food. A few more days he even stay out when us other people is on the porch.

"Guess you can shoot that gopher about any time you want to," Judy say to Mr. Whitey one evening.

He smile his big wide smile and look like he don't for sure know what to do with his hands. "He don't seem to be near as much of a pest as he was, besides I don't think the little boy would like it." He smile again and laugh and his big red face be all covered in sweat.

It easy for me to tell by the way Mr. Whitey is acting that he sure do like Judy Powderface. I go to bed early, usually, leave them drink tea in the kitchen. Emmanuel been given a bedroom upstairs, Judy got the room next to mine, and Mr. Whitey have the big room across the hall.

When they is alone he talk nice to Judy, and it seem to me that Mr. Whitey be almost shy around her, but I guess that couldn't be. I never knew any white people that was shy, only Indians. What could white people have to be shy about?

Judy be kind of nervous when he talk about how much money he got in the bank and how he figure to make lots of improvement to the farm if Judy going to stay around and help him. I can tell by Judy's voice that everything be okay with her. Guess she think about living with her uncle where there be about ten people for two rooms. When I think about it I guess Judy Powderface could do a lot worse for herself.

Saturday, Mr. Whitey say, we all going to town for the day, and he go and clean all the junk out of the back of his '67 Plymouth Fury two door. Then he take a tub of hot water into his room and in an hour or so he come out rub a towel on his big round face. He got on a black shirt have a big red flower painted on it and a pair of cream-coloured cord pants. He got on his hand-tooled belt with a silver buckle look like a spider, that he say come all the way from Mexico, and his cowboy boots been shined real good. He shaved his face until it be red as a radish and then he put on a whole lot of Aqua Velva.

Everybody pretty happy on the trip to town, I even seen Little Emmanuel smile once. He got a box full of mice in his room. I seen him talk to them and I pretty sure that they listen. I ask Judy is it be okay if I leave word for Eathen to drive Mad Etta out on Sunday to have a look at the way Little Emmanuel handle animals. If he keep up this way he make a fine medicine man someday. Mad Etta been try to teach me some of the secret of be a medicine man but I don't fool myslf that I got any real powers like Emmanuel seem to have. On the way to town Mr. Whitey sing along with the radio in a deep flat voice.

We pull up in front of the Co-op Store and Mr. Whitey give Judy $80, tell her to buy whatever groceries she think we need and anything else she might like, like a dress or something. He be real shy when he tell her this and look all the time at the steering wheel.

"You want to go shoot a game of pool?" I say to Mr. Whitey after we been to the paint store buy up seven gallons of white paint for the outside of the house. Soon as we get in the pool hall I'm sure sorry I asked him cause there be a bunch of bad characters shoot eight ball and drink Cokes. There be Wade Gaskell and the Iverson brothers, and some other guys like them who don't like anybody but themselves.

"Hear you going native, Whitey," one of them say as soon as we set up on our table. Mr. Whitey do his inbreathing laugh and give them a shrug of his shoulders, but his face be all of a sudden covered in sweat.

"They tell us you got a little dark meat living with you," Wade Gaskell say. "Nothing like a squaw to keep you warm, eh Whitey?" and he punch Mr. Whitey's arm real hard.

I don't understand why these young guys talk so rude to Mr. Whitey, cause he be about 40 and they don't usually be so smart with older men.

"Tell us what it's like, Whitey. I hear that squaw you got is really hot stuff. My brother says he had her after a dance down at Hobbema and that she really knows how to move it," Lew Iverson says. His brother just smile and nod.

Mr. Whitey try to just look at the pool table. He do his inbreathing laugh and shake his head.

"Don't tell me you're not getting any? Jesus, you won't keep a squaw around for long like that." Then Wade Gaskell say to his friends, "I wonder if old Whitey would know what to do with it if it walked up and bit him?" and they all laugh real loud.

Mr. Whitey stayed and finished the game but them guys kept tease him most of the time. By the time we leave his shirt be soaked to his back and belly and he have to wipe his face with his handkerchief two or three times.

"They're mean dudes, Mr. Whitey," I say to him. "Don't pay no attention to what they say. Wade's brother did a murder here a couple of years ago. They're all that kind of guys." But Mr. Whitey just stare straight ahead as we walk back to the car.

Judy is wait for us, all smiles, at the Co-op Store. She be excited to tell us about the good buys she got and she give back to Mr. Whitey must be $30 of what he gave her.

Mr. Whitey hardly say nothing and he got a big thick V right in between his eyebrows that he make by squinting his eyes like he thinking real hard to remember something.

We all go to the Gold Nugget Café across from the Canadian Legion. We have deluxe hamburgers and chips with gravy. I try to make some jokes to get Mr. Whitey to feel better and finally he laugh a little. He pour about half a bottle of ketchup on his chips and a couple of times he spill some right on the big red flower on his shirt. He say he watering the flower and we all have a good laugh about that, even Little Emmanuel. Then Mr. Whitey, still look worried but not so much, take us all to the Wheatlands Theatre for the early show. Him and me sure laugh at that cartoon of that there Roadrunner Bird and the poor old coyote who always get rocks dropped on him. Emmanuel be more interested in looking at the ceiling which got a whole lot of tiny lights look like stars on a clear night.

On the way back to the farm I ride in the back seat with Little Emmanuel and he go to sleep beside me, roll over and lay with his head on my knee. Judy sit over close to Mr. Whitey and kind of rest her head on his shoulder. She say a couple or three times about how much she enjoy herself and tell Mr. Whitey what a good man he is. When we get to the farm I carry Little Emmanuel upstairs and put him in his bed and then I go to my room. Judy makes tea but I don't hear hardly no talk from Mr. Whitey, and I sure surprised when I hear him get up and walk heavy to his bedroom without even say goodnight.

In the middle of the night I get waked up by a lot of noise come from Judy Powderface's bedroom.

"All you had to do was ask," I hear her say, her voice all muffled like maybe she got her hands in front of her face. "You figure cause I'm Indian you don't have to ask."

Mr. Whitey mumble something that I don't hear.

"No," say Judy Powderface pretty loud, and then a couple more times. It ain't the kind of no that telling him to stop something, but the kind that means she ain't gonna do something.

Then I hear Mr. Whitey do his inbreathing laugh, the bed creak, and his big bare feet slap the linoleum back to his room.

When I get up in the morning Judy and Emmanuel's cardboard boxes be packed and sitting by the door. She see me look at the boxes.

"When Eathen bring Mad Etta up to see Emmanuel, we're going back to the reserve with them."

I don't know if she expect me to ask why or not, but I don't.

Half an hour or so later I just coming up from feed the chickens when I hear Mr. Whitey's gun shooting.

"One down and a couple to go," he say to me as I come round the corner of the house, and he kind of say it to Judy Powderface too, who be come to the screen door see what the shooting is all about. Little Emmanel still sit cross-legged in front of the gopher hole, his hand still hold out some green stuff. Right in front of his hand the gopher lay dead where Mr. Whitey put about three bullets in him.

Emmanuel don't cry or nothing. He just reach down and pick up the dead gopher. He hold it in his little black hands that be dark and shiny as polished furniture in the lobby of the Alice Hotel in Wetaskiwin, and turn his head slow to look at Mr. Whitey. The look on Emmanuel's face be so fierce that it even scare me a little bit.

Judy Powderface look at me in a way that sort of ask what she should do, but I don't know. Mr. Whitey lean his rifle against the porch railing, take a step back and laugh that inbreathing laugh of his.

"It's only a gopher," he say real low. His face be awful red and covered with sweat and there be big wet spots under each arm of his blue shirt. Little Emmanuel just keep looking at him and he hold the gopher against his own chest and it make its own kind of stains on him. All I know is I wouldn't want to be Mr. Whitey Bremner today, not for all the things in the world that I can think of.

bones

After they carted Redwater Jones' bones off to the Glenbow Museum place in Calgary, we all sit around Blind Louis Coyote's cabin on the reserve and talk about it some, especially Bedelia Coyote who figure we should do something about it. She remind us that us guys got an organization— The Hobbema Chapter of The Ermineskin Warrior Society —what was started for us by the American Indian Movement.

A name like that be kind of exciting, make us think of war parties and do brave things. Bedelia say that we should go down to that museum place and demand that they give us back the bones so we can bury them in the Indian cemetery or at least keep them guys from put Redwater Jones on display like something from a zoo.

Bedelia Coyote is short, heavy-set, and she got long black

hair parted down the middle. Her hair is coarse and when I look down on top of her head it look like she got a line painted with white paint divide the two halves of her hair. She got a wide, soft nose, full lips and big mouthful of teeth. Bedelia believe in this here women's rights stuff and she get that MS magazine delivered to her along with a lot of mail from something called Feminist News Service, and she go around calling the other girls sister even though they ain't related. Being a woman is pretty bad Bedelia say, being a poor woman is worse, but being a poor Indian woman is worst of all.

We say maybe we gonna do something about it but not right now.

Bedelia don't give up easy and she follow us guys down to the pool hall at Hobbema where she grab the pink ball off the table and bounce it down to the far end of the hall to get us to pay attention to her.

What cause all the trouble was that a carload of archaeologists come snoop around the reserve one day. They got permission from Indian Affairs Department to dig in a place where some new houses being built. That would of been okay probably but they get lost on the way there, get their car stuck and while they trying to dig it out find the bones of an Indian been dead a long time.

Since they dig him up from a place where they not supposed to be we try and keep them from taking the bones away. But Chief Tom Crow-eye, who rather be white than Indian, smile all over them archaeologists, tell them about his run for the Conservative Party in the next election and tell them take away whatever they want.

Me and Bedelia and my friend Frank Fence-post is name that Indian Redwater Jones cause where they found his bones was in a ditch of red clay.

"Why don't you guys get off your asses and do something?" Bedelia yell at us. "If we all go down there and ask for them bones back they have to give them to us."

"Most of us guys is pretty shy about meet up with Government people," I explain.

"Yeah, if we could maybe fist fight them for the bones it make everything okay," say Frank.

"If you guys don't go then I go by myself. Tell everyone the Ermineskin Warrior Society be a bunch of old men too tired to fight for the bones of their brother."

Next day we borrow Louis Coyote's pickup truck and six of us guys and Bedelia Coyote go to Calgary to the Glenbow Institute.

Boy, it be one big place and even Bedelia is not very brave when we get there. I'm the only one been there before so I take them up to where a Mr. Hugh Dempsey is have his office. He be a man who helped me learn some Indian history one time. Mr. Dempsey got a grey suit and a kind face. He shake hands on all of us and say he don't know nothing about Redwater Jones but he call up the men who do and get them to have a meeting with us.

Mr. Dempsey be a white man but he got an Indian wife and he have a picture of her right up on his desk to show that he ain't ashamed to have her.

We get taken into a conference room with a long wood table got glass over the top of it. The walls be painted pale purple on one side and yellow on the other and the ceiling look like a big plastic ice-cube tray that they sell at Metropolitan Store, only it be full of white light bulbs.

There is four guys in suits and ties, each have puffy cheeks and small eyes. Mr. Dempsey wish us luck and go off to his own office, but first he tell the other men he wishes they listen close to what we say.

All these fancy rooms make us real nervous. I bet the museum men be nervous and feel out of place if they was to meet with us in the beer parlour of the Queen's Hotel in Calgary, which is the place downtown where all the Indians hang around.

We tell them as polite as we know how that them archaeologists dig up the bones of the man we call Redwater Jones on a part of the reserve where they ain't supposed to be. So we figure they shouldn't have hauled the bones off the reserve and they should give them back to us so we can take and bury them proper.

The men don't take long to tell us that them bones be historical objects and they got a right to keep them cause they come under the Indian Artifacts Act or something like that. They wave around a printed paper and give it to me cause I the one who reads best, but that printing be all full of whereases and other big Government words. As near as I can see it worded so the Government can do whatever it wants which is what it always does anyway. Sure wish we could print up rules and make them into laws the way the Government does.

Then Bedelia Coyote speak up and tell them, "Hey, we going to one of these days go up to maybe the Mount Pleasant Cemetery in Edmonton—one of them white man burial grounds—and dig around for some white man artifacts. We figure we start up a white-man museum at Hobbema, maybe in the empty building used to be the McLeod Hardware Store what went broke. We set knives and forks and broken bottles around on shelves and boy, when we dig up a dead white man we gonna glue all his bones together and put him out for tourists to see every summer and for school kids come look at and study about."

Boy them white men sure get excited as Bedelia talk.

"Hey, Silas," Frank Fence-post whisper to me, "if Bedelia talks much longer them guys gonna be red enough to be Indians."

"There are laws against desecrating graves," one of the suits tells us in a voice like a minister. "Should you even consider taking such action we would respond with every legal weapon at our disposal."

This is exactly what Bedelia want them to say. "Then how come there is no law to keep people from dig up our graves on the reserve?"

"That's different," they say. "We are digging in the name of history. Besides you're only . . ." and he stop without finishing the sentence.

"We only gonna dig up graves of people who dies before maybe 1910. We can dig in the name of history too," say

Bedelia. Frank and Rufus and the rest of us guys slap our hands on the glass table top to show we agree with her.

We argue as good as we can but they is the Government and we is Indians so it be pretty easy to figure out what going to happen.

We go down to the Queen's Hotel and have us a few beers and I guess most of us willing to forget the whole thing, but not Bedelia.

"What kind of Warrior Society are you guys anyway?" she say to us. "You never hear of a raiding party? If you guys don't do something I get me a gun and go back there and hold them up."

It sure make us guys feel pretty small to hear her talk that way. We don't want people to think we be like Chief Tom who left his wife on the reserve and live with his girlfriend in Wetaskiwin in an apartment got a sauna bath and a swimming pool. And too we don't want Bedelia should get herself in trouble so we drive back out to Glenbow. Mr. Dempsey told us that Redwater Jones be in a place called cataloguing. In the lobby of the Glenbow I read the big building directory on the wall then I go down to the basement to the cataloguing department. I take me a deep breath and walk right in like I supposed to be there.

"Mr. Dempsey sent me down for the bones from the Ermineskin Reserve at Hobbema," I say. "He want to show them to the people at the meeting so they can see they being looked after okay."

The guy go and get three green plastic bags.

"Sign here," he say and push a white form at me.

I sign it, Redwater Jones.

Outside, Frank he back the truck right over a parking meter he be in such a hurry to get away. We sure pretty excited cause the Ermineskin Warrior Society done its first raid. I change places with Frank as we drive up the highway toward Hobbema cause Frank he ain't got no driver's licence.

We figure we gonna put Redwater Jones up on a platform, let the air get at his bones the way old-time Indians

19

used to do with their dead people.

"Did our tribe used to really do that?" Bedelia ask.

I don't know for sure and neither do anyone else but we all seen it done in the movie *Jeremiah Johnson* that showed at the Wheatlands Theatre in Wetaskiwin.

Ain't hardly anyone around that remembers the old customs no more. I stop by and ask our medicine lady, Mad Etta, if she thinks we put our dead up in trees. She say she think we did a long time ago but she not sure.

"Have to build a platform out of big logs to hold Etta," she say and laugh and laugh, shake like a water bed I seen in a furniture store in Edmonton one time. Etta she weigh about 300 pounds and over to the Alice Hotel in Wetaskiwin they got two chairs wired together and braced with two-by-fours so Etta can drink beer and not bust up the furniture.

Next morning, Bedelia, me, Frank and Rufus Firstrider, go way back in the bush and with small logs and limbs we build a platform in the trees to hold Redwater Jones. We got those bags of bones hang on a rope in Sam Standing-at-the-door's cream well, which be about the last place we figure the RCMP to look if they come around.

It snowed in the night and everything be white, the poplar trees look all silvery against the sky and our voices seem to carry a long way even when we speak soft. Frank he want to bring a chain-saw to cut the trees for the platform, but me and Bedelia say no, old-time Indians don't have no chain-saws, we got to do this with our own hands.

"What if this here guy ain't Indian?" Frank say.

Bedelia's face look surprised like she ain't thought of that before.

"He could be white. That land weren't even reserve when they say he died. We don't even know if he was a he," Frank keep on.

Bedelia be silent for a while, pull hard at a piece of dead-fall. "When you get right down to the bones I guess it don't make so much difference," she say.

That night we head out to the platform, get as close as we can with Louis Coyote's pickup. The bones be in the back of the truck and we got Mad Etta in the back of the truck too, under her tarpaulin, look like we carry maybe a big statue. She be pretty good for extra weight in case the truck start to get stuck in the snow. When we get out of the truck there be some cigarette smoke come from around the edge of the tarp, so we know Mad Etta be under there and okay.

We still over half a mile from where we build the platform. We walk along single file through the poplar and willow trees. The snow is fall in big soft flakes like owl feathers.

Me and Frank and Bedelia each got one of the slippery bags with bones in it. The snow be too soft to crunch and about all you can hear is Mad Etta wheeze some cause she not used to walk for such a long time. I see a flake big as a postage stamp land right on Mad Etta's big flat nose.

Etta she know the old-time death songs of our people and she start up to chant some, first soft as the voice of a small animal then rise up slow to the scream of the hawk. We take up the rhythm of her voice and we pretty soon move along the snowy trail like dancers.

pit lamping

For Mario M. Martinelli

Me and my friend Frank Fence-post is having a beer at the Alice Hotel bar when Philip Eagle come busting in. He just about walk through the door without opening it he is so excited to tell somebody his news that he got himself a real good job.

"Lumber camp couple of hundred miles north of Fort St. John. Promise me six months steady work, seven days a week if I want it. I leave day after tomorrow."

Well Frank and me we shake his hand and slap his back and order up a round of drinks. We make so much noise the waiter come over and tell us to be more quiet.

Philip Eagle be one of the guys who go to the Technical School at Wetaskiwin with us. He learns all about fix big engines and he do it so good that now he got this job. And, boy, it sure pays good money too.

Only thing worries me is that it be so far away, must be 500 miles or more, and I sure wonder how Philip Eagle's girlfriend Marian Lizotte going to act about his going away. Philip and Marion been together for maybe a year or so.

"You gonna take Marion with you?" I ask him.

"Naw, got no place for women at the camp. She'll be okay. I'll send her lots of bread."

I'm pretty sure that it ain't gonna be bread that Marion cares about. Marion ain't all that pretty but she got about the nicest eyes I ever seen. They be light brown and she got lashes that come all the way down and touch on her cheeks. Those eyes be kind of big for her face and sometimes I be able to see myself reflected in them when she is talking right at me.

Us and Philip drink beer for a while.

I keep trying to get him to think about Marion but he ain't much interested. Me and Marion have had some serious talks a couple of times and because of what she told me, it sure worries me now that Philip going to up and leave her.

"Aren't you going to be lonesome up there all alone? Probably won't be no other Indians around."

Philip just laugh a little. "I'll get along. It'll be like doing hard time. But the money'll be worth it. I'll get me a new car and a rifle."

Philip like to pretend that he be a pretty tough guy. He picks up words from the guys who been in jail and he like to give people he don't know the idea that he been in jail too. He never been in trouble though, except one time he got arrested by the game wardens of the Government Lands and Forests Department. Him and a couple of white guys got caught pit lamping. They was out in the middle of the night hooting across a stubble field chasing down a deer in the white guys' jeep. After a day or so they let Philip go cause he was just along for the ride and don't mean nobody no harm. They fine those white guys about a thousand dollars each though and take away their jeep with the big spotlight and their guns so that they never get them back again.

I don't know why hunting at night is called pit lamping but I seen a deer once that was run down by some guys in a pickup truck. The deer weren't a very big one. Guess it just run as far as it could go and laid down to die right along the edge of the road. I went up to look at it close but it just laid there its sides going up and down like a movie they showed us at the Technical School of a heart operation. I could only see one eye on account of the position it was laying in but the moonlight shine right down into that eye with a kind of blue glow like railroad tracks. There be so much fear in that eye that I'm afraid it gonna explode all over me, and I turn away quick.

"Why don't we get us a dozen beers and go back to my place?" Philip says. "I ain't told Marion yet that I got the job."

Philip is thin built and his shoulders stoop a little bit, he got long dark hair that hang like it kind of tired. He have a pretty long nose and a lot of pox marks on his cheeks. His hands is real long and slim and the colour of rungs in a varnished rocking chair I seen one time. He got on a denim jacket and jeans and yellow work boots laced up past his ankles.

Frank he say he going over to the Legion Bar see if he can find Connie Bigcharles who be a girl he like for his girl-friend except that she don't like him. We tease Frank about that some and he say to us some words in Cree and go walk out the door. Pretty hard to make into English but it some-thing like, "Go saw off your nose with a chain-saw."

Philip and me walk over to his place and down the side stairs to the door to his rooms. It snowing quite heavy, but real light puffy flakes that hang in our hair and that I some-times breathe up my nose like dandelion fluff.

"Silas," he say to me, "why don't you phone a message to Sadie. She can get a ride up from the reserve and we can make a party tonight." Sadie One-wound is my girlfriend. We gonna get married sometime.

Philip bust through the door to his place just like he do at the bar. "Hey, Babe, I got me a job," he yell. Marion poke her head around the corner into the kitchen, then come throw her arms around Philip's neck and kiss him big.

She don't stay happy for long though, cause Philip he tell her right off that it be a long way away and that he going there alone. It easy for me to see that Marion is pretty shook up but she try her best to be happy cause Philip is happy. Marion is a little bit plump and she got a round face with freckles on her cheeks like I seen on the wings of some butterflies. Aren't many Indian girls got freckles. She be wearing a white sweater that look new, clean jeans and slippers made out of soft yellow wool.

Philip insist that we gonna make a party, and he don't take no as an answer.

"I'm going down to the corner and phone the pool hall at Hobbema. They can send one of the kids up to tell Sadie that we want her in town," and before anyone can argue with him he's gone, waving his bottle of beer in his hand as he go out the door.

Marion sits down across the kitchen table from me and lights up a cigarette. Her eyes look like glasses of water been filled right to the very top.

Their apartment is really tiny but Marion sure know how to make it a nice place. Some couples I know live in rooms like this but it don't seem to be a place you'd want to stay. Everything be bare and look cold even if the weather be hot.

Marion got everything done up bright: there be yellow curtains on the window and a plant with furry-looking leaves. She been around to the carpet store in Wetaskiwin and got them to give her the leftover pieces. She glued them to the wall in the living-room looks like a big shield with maybe a picture in it or maybe not. The couch is old but she knitted bright-coloured covers for the arms and back. She put record covers in a pattern all over one wall and hang glass things from the ceiling that make tinkle sounds when they rub together. Their house is a pretty nice place to be and when I look around I figure that Philip Eagle be one lucky guy.

"How can I be happy for him, Silas, when what make him so happy is to be leaving me?"

"I don't think Philip means you no harm," I say. "He be the first Indian guy from the Tech School to get a real good job doing what he been trained to do. He got to pretty well take what gets offered him."

Marion's table be pretty old and beat up but it sure is clean and she got white place mats on the table have yellow daisies all around the edges. Marion just look at me for a minute and then her eyes overflow some. She don't make no crying sounds, just some tears come out and sit on her cheeks, then slide down.

"He could work here if he wanted to."

"You sure?"

"They wanted him down at the Allis-Chalmers Tractor Store. Floyd Coyote walked over here on his lunch hour today to find out why Philip turned down that job after Floyd went to so much trouble to get his boss to hire him. When he first come in with you tonight I figured that he'd changed his mind. I was so happy, Silas, I don't want to be alone ..." She stop then and sniff some.

Marion, she have a pretty bad life. No father, and her mother live mostly at the beer parlour of the Canadian Legion. Marion been in and out of the Catholic Orphanage here at Wetaskiwin and a whole lot of foster homes all her life. Most girls that have a life like hers end up just like their mother, but Marion work really hard not to be a bad girl.

"Silas, I never have nothing in my life until Philip come along. He love me so good and make me feel like he need me. Why does he want to go away from me?"

Boy, I sure wish maybe I was someplace else. I wish that there was some way to make sad people feel better. I'm pretty glad to hear Philip come bang back down the steps.

Eathen Firstrider was at the pool hall. He's gonna get Blind Louis' pickup and drive Sadie up here in an hour or so. He's gonna bring a girl too, so we'll all make a big party to celebrate my job."

He didn't notice Marion's tears.

"Hey, Babe," he say, "Silas is out of beer and that walk make me thirsty too."

Marion go to the fridge and get us each a beer. Hers is still on the table and she ain't touched it at all.

Philip be busy talk about all the things that he got to do before he goes away. Marion tries to interrupt a couple of times but he don't notice that anyone but him is talking. She wait quiet for her chance and then she say, "Philip, would there be time for us to get married before you go?"

"No," he say right away. "We'd have to go to Edmonton to get the licence and all that and then wait three days or something." He sees Marion's face kind of breaking up and add, "Hell, when I get back we'll have a real blow-out. Put on a potlatch like the old-time Indians did. We have us a real wedding. Everybody be drunk for a week."

I don't think that make Marion feel much better, cause right after, Philip he go back to talking about his plans for go away. Then he remember that it is a Thursday night and that the stores be open late.

"Let's run down to Field's Store before Eathen gets here. I got to get some steel-toed boots and some wrenches and stuff." He already finished his beer and be half-way to the door.

"You go ahead," I say. "I think I stay and talk to Marion. I like to be here when Sadie comes."

"Hey, Partner, you're with me, remember," Philip says, and pulls me up from my chair.

"It's okay, Silas," Marion says. "I think I take me a bath," and she smile at us with her face but the look in her eyes make me turn for the door, even though I know that's not what I should do. She come around the table to kiss Philip but he already got his back turned to start up the stairs.

I not very good company for Philip as we walk downtown. He buys a pair of boots at the Field Department Store. Then we go walk around the McLeod Hardware.

I don't know whether I should tell Philip or not, but like

I've said me and Marion have some serious talks a couple of times.

"I was fourteen the first time I try to kill myself," she say to me one time, and she go on to tell me about all the bad things that happen to her until she meet up with Philip. "Philip don' know," she say to me, "and I know I can trust you not to tell him."

I never know what to say to people who tell me stuff like that. Marion look over at me across the table to see what I going to say. I try to be busy stir the sugar and milk into my coffee and I make out like what she said was maybe about the weather. I think that's maybe why people tell me so many secrets: I just listen and don't tell them whether they is right or wrong, even if they ask me.

"Marion loves you a lot," I say to Philip.

"Yeah, she's a pretty good old lady."

"You got to be kind of careful with her, Philip. She be the kind of girl that break easy . . . like pretty dishes . . ."

Philip don't even hear me say that. He got him a box of wrenches down off a shelf and he is busy fitting the parts together.

On the way back we stop off at the Alice Hotel and each of us buy a box of beer. There in the bar is Frank Fence-post sit with his arm around the shoulder of Connie Bigcharles. He smile at us like he just picked somebody's pocket and don't get caught. He yells us over to their table and we invite them back to Philip's. Frank goes and gets them a case of beer too.

When we get to Philip's place Louis Coyote's pickup is parked in front. It got Eathen Firstrider, Julie Scar and my girlfriend Sadie One-wound in it.

"We figured you guys would be back pretty soon," Eathen says. "Where's Marion?"

"In the house."

"No she ain't. We banged on the door. The lights are all off and the door's locked."

"She must of gone someplace," says Philip.

We all go around the side of the house. About the only

sound is the beer bottles clinking in their boxes. Philip unlocks the door. Right away we get inside I hear the water running in the bathroom, even before Philip turns on the kitchen light. The bathroom door is locked and Marion don't answer. I gonna break it in but the others don't want me to. Landlords get awful uptight about things like that especially if it be Indians live in a place.

I finally do bust it open.

Guess Marion she figure she have to be neat and clean even if she do something terrible to herself. What she done is knelt down by the bath tub, turned the water on, and cut her wrists with a razor blade. Most of the blood been washed away except for some that splashed up on the side in drops that make a pattern like a handful of red flowers.

I have to yell at Philip about three times before he run out to phone an ambulance.

The ambulance is white and shiny like the sinks and bath tubs they have in hotels. There be two flashers on top, one turn each way, make blood-coloured light over all the houses and the snowy street.

The ambulance guys lay Marion on a stretcher that got wheels. Her eyes are closed, the long lashes touching her cheeks. There be big blood spots on her white sweater and the blood on the legs of her jeans look dark like rain. They bandaged her wrists so it look like she got clean cuffs on her sweater, and you have to look awful close to see if she breathing or not.

Philip just sit at the kitchen table, turn a beer bottle round and round in his dark hands and pick some at the label. It sure seem funny to me that Marion look so small on that stretcher. She seem like not much more than a little girl.

The guys carry her up the stairs and wheel her along the sidewalk out to the ambulance. The red lights splash all over, and the eyes of people who stand around glint red out of the darkness. The inside of the ambulance look like an oven with the lights on, and they push Marion right up into the middle of all that light.

canadian culture

They come snoop around the reserve one afternoon in the late summer, a whole carload of them, three in the front seat, three in the back. Their car look like a tank I seen in an army movie once, got cameras poked out of all the windows the way hunters have guns. Anytime you see a car on the reserve with six white people in it, all look like they just had their faces washed with a stiff washcloth, it sure don't mean anything but trouble.

Me and my friend Frank Fence-post and our girlfriends, Sadie One-wound and Connie Bigcharles is walking kind of slow on the corduroy road through the slough, on our way down to the pool hall at Hobbema. That car full of white people pull up and, boy, two or three of them jump out and point their machine-gun-looking cameras at us. They move real quick just like policemans do when they come to arrest people. Frank put his hands on the roof of the car, spread his feet and yell, "Police brutality," like us guys do when the RCMP come around look for moonshine or stolen car parts.

"We didn't mean to scare you," say the lady who drive the car. Then she ask us for direction to the Blue Quills Hall. She tell us she heard that Chief Tom Crow-eye suppose to be down there and they want to see him cause they maybe going to make a movie show all about us Indians here at Hobbema.

"For five dollars each we show you which way it is," say Frank.

One of the men is about 6′ 4″ got a droopy yellow moustache and look like he could dig a basement with his bare hands. He got the barrel end of his camera pointed right at Frank's nose, and he at the same time look down on the top of Frank's head.

"Two dollars each," say Frank, while all six of them cameras whir like partridge drum around in the underbrush.

"Plain two dollars," say Frank. The big guy just shake his head.

"You ain't gonna pay us at all, are you, partner?" The big guy just keep on shake his head.

We say okay we tell them which way if they just give us a cigarette each. Connie Bigcharles ask one of the guys if he want her to unbutton her shirt some, and she make sexy eyes at him until he back away. Sadie kind of hides behind me cause she be shy with white peoples.

We give them real serious directions that going to get their car stuck in a slough. Guess though that we laugh too much among ourselves when we doing it, cause the lady who driving say, "Don't you try to con us. I know how to speak your language."

"Go fry your boots and eat them for lunch," Frank say to her in Cree.

She look blank. She be about thirty, got kind of gold-coloured hair and be wearing tight blue jeans, yellow cowboy boots, a checkered shirt, gold-rimmed glasses, and smoke one of them ladies' cigarettes that be only half as big around as ordinary ones.

"What did I say?" Frank ask her.

"You talked too fast for me."

Then Frank he get a look of mischief in his eye and he tell her real slow in Cree about some things he think her and him could do to each other in bed.

Connie Bigcharles give Frank a hard hit on the arm.

"I guess maybe I don't understand as well as I thought I did," the lady say. "It was only a two-week crash course." But I can tell by look at her that she understand some of what Frank say to her, cause her face get about the same colour as the red part of her shirt.

"For twenty dollars I teach you what it was I said," Frank say, and he grin to show his couple of missing teeth and be real proud of himself. He step toward her but she jump back in that car real quick and so do the whole bunch of them, though the driver lady give Frank a pretty sharp look and she drag real deep on that cigarette of hers.

After they drive off, we turn around and head back for our cabins. We figure they be up there pretty soon, look for somebody to unstuck their car. And about an hour later they are. All six come up single file, three shoot film on each side of the road. I put on my cherry-coloured western shirt and my ten gallon black felt hat with the feather and leather braid on it, and boy, it feel pretty good have all those cameras point at me. I'd like someday to be this here Donny Osmond fellow on TV.

"For thirty dollars we get us a truck and pull you out," we tell them.

"Go straight to hell," the big guy tell us, and want to know who's got a telephone for call a tow truck.

"Nearest phone is down to Hobbema, and the tow truck won't come out here to the reserve no matter how white you are."

"Why not?" the driver lady say.

"Last time they come out here was maybe three years ago. Somebody invite the driver in for a drink of moonshine while somebody else strip the truck right down to the ground."

"We're going to Hobbema anyway," they say.

"Cost you fifty dollars when you get back," we tell them. And we hold them to it too, in advance, when they plod up to the cabins all tired and sweaty from the long walk down and back. We go get Blind Louis pickup truck and a long piece of cable that we borrow without asking from the Alberta Government Telephones, and we be all ready to pull their car out. But when we get to the slough, the hood be up on the car, and everything that come loose quick, including all four wheels and the spare tire, they all be gone.

They is all for go call the police right away. We sure don't want that. Indians and RCMP be like oil and water, don't mix at all.

I decide to try and bluff them.

"RCMP like tow truck, don't come out to the reserve either." Frank catch on quick to what I doing.

"You go see Chief Tom Crow-eye," he say. "The chief be rich. He buy you guys some new wheels and stuff."

"Where is this Blue Quills Hall?" the lady driver whose name is Marcia, is say.

"About two miles back, that way," we tell her.

"Then you gave us the wrong directions," she yell.

"We here on the reserve don't speak or understand very much English," I say, real slow and clear as I know how, and I try not to break up with laughter the way Frank and Connie do.

We load all them movie peoples in the back of the truck and I take them about 60 mph over the corduroy road down to Blue Quills. Frank look back and say that they bounce around like popcorn in the back of the truck.

Chief Tom we know be on the reserve today. He hardly ever is, but today there is a Conservative Party meeting down at the hall and Chief Tom be there cause he want the Indians to vote on him in the next election.

At the hall we find Chief Tom in his suit and tie, have tea with the women's club. My Ma, Suzie Ermineskin, and our

33

medicine lady, Mad Etta, be there too.

"You think Poundmaker would believe that that be an Indian chief?" say Frank, looking at Chief Tom drink tea and make little jokes with the ladies.

Chief Tom he don't live on the reserve no more. He left his wife and him and his girlfriend got an apartment in Wetaskiwin. Tom Crow-eye figure that someday he probably gonna be a white man.

Since being the chief of us Indians and then being in that there politics, if there is one thing Chief Tom learn to recognize, it is a camera. Must seem like the happy hunting ground to him when he see six white people, each with a running camera, coming toward him.. He got on his shiny blue suit, and red, white and blue tie. His hair be styled by a beauty parlour for men. His girlfriend, Samantha Yellow-knees, make him go get his teeth polished by a dentist so they shine just like the white sinks in the men's room of the new hotels in Edmonton.

Well, he just about walk right over us Indians to get to shake hands with them white movie men, welcome them to Hobbema and to Blue Quills, and let them know he be running for the Conservative Party in the next election and be a personal friend of Premier Lougheed. Some of the movie people seem kind of disappointed that the chief look like he do, and be more interested in photo Mad Etta, who must of been out on a doctor call before she came to the meeting, cause she wearing some war paint and got fox tails tied down both sleeves of her five-flour-sack dress. Mad Etta be a really big lady. Over to the beer parlour of the Alice Hotel in Wetaskiwin they got two chairs wired together and braced with two-by-fours so that Mad Etta can drink beer and not bust up the furniture.

Them white people ain't so dumb as you would think. They all act awful impressed at meet a real live Indian chief, keep their cameras run on him, and tell how much they like Premier Lougheed and how they figure Chief Tom make a great member of parliament.

"We are delighted to have you here," he tell them quite

34

a few times, and he get more delighted all the time as they tell him they probably gonna make a movie here at Hobbema.

The guy with the droopy moustache is called Allen Decker and he used to one time play football for the Baltimore Colts. He flex up his muscles when he tell us this. The driver lady's name is Marcia Cartwright and she come all the way from Los Angeles. The short, dark guy with no hair and blue glasses like this here Elton John singer, is called Morty Goldfinch and come from New York. The other three camera peoples come all the way from Italy to make the movie to take back with them, and the whole bunch of them been sent out here by Culture Canada.

Chief Tom claim he know a whole lot about Culture Canada and he tell them too that he reading a book on parliamentary procedure so he know how to act when he get elected to the Government. Then he pledge co-operation with them on behalf of all of us, all of Alberta and everyone else he can think of. It kind of make me wonder that even though this is called Culture Canada, there don't seem to be a Canadian have nothing to do with it. But I guess that is just the way the Government be.

"While we're being friendly," say Mr. Decker the football player, "these boys," and he point his middle finger, look like a foot-long hot dog, at me and Frank, "gave us wrong directions, charged us fifty dollars to tow our car, and then, while we were away, some of their friends stripped our car."

"Not our friends," say Frank. "We do our own stealing."

"The boys say you'll pay for our losses," Decker go on. Well, Chief Tom's face get a look like he been bit on the ass by a big dog. We all know that Chief Tom be real good at hand out advice, but when it come to money, if he were out in the desert he want to rent a dying man his sweat.

Chief Tom pull back his lips and smile even though it hurts him to. Then he give us about a ten minute lecture on what he call public relations. He make us hand back the fifty dollars, and make us promise to get back the car parts or he personal call in the RCMP and see that we maybe go to jail for steal those parts. Guess that what it mean to be a politician. Somebody ask you for money and you see that somebody else pay it.

While the movie people sit down for tea we go over to Hobbema, and sure enough there be Gordon Tailfeathers, David One-wound, and quite a few other guys hang around the Texaco Service Station. They already sold the air-cleaner, the jack, and three of the wheels, to tourists who stop for gas, and they was just talk about go back for the seats and maybe a door or two.

We load Donald and Gordon and a whole bunch of kids into the truck and drive back to where that pale green Chev with Culture Canada in white letter on the side, is sitting.

I don't understand this here Culture Canada. When class start again in the fall I get Mr. Nichols, my counselor at the Tech School to explain it to me. I remember one time when I be really sick with a bad throat, and Mad Etta be away somewhere, I go to the white doctor in Wetaskiwin and he rub a stick down my throat to catch some germs, and say that be a culture. Can't see no connection between the two.

We can't put back enough parts to get the engine to run, and besides we only got two wheels. We argue some about whether to put the wheels on the front or the back. It be pretty hard whatever way we do it cause the guys already sold the jack and Louis' pickup never had one. What we do is we all heave on the car, tip it over on its side, and we put one wheel on the back, then we figure to tip it on its feet and over on the other side, that way get both back wheels on. What happen, though is we push too hard the second time, roll the car right over on its side and on to its roof. When it be on its roof in the ditch it be just too heavy for us to get right-side up again. We know them Culture Canada people sure gonna be mad if we come back without their car, so what we do is tie that there cable to the axle and tow it down the road on its roof. It slide pretty bad that way and skid off in the ditch and up against trees a lot, even though Frank sit upside-down inside and work the brake pedal some. Finally, though, we get it down to the Hobbema Texaco Garage. The body pretty well shot to hell, but we figure it run okay with just a few parts. Them guys shouldn't care that the windows all broke cause they have them open most of the time anyway.

We figure Mr. Decker not gonna be very happy but we sure don't think he gonna be so mad he hit Frank in the nose the way he do. Decker, Mr. Goldfinch and Miss Cartwright ain't very happy with what we done to their car. Decker say he wonder if they got the Ku Klux Klan here in Alberta, and if they don't, why they don't. Goldfinch take off his blue glasses, look at Decker from white eye holes and say, "I'm Jewish."

I don't understand the whole thing.

It was when Frank ask Decker for our fifty dollars back for tow the car into town, that Decker punch Frank square in the nose, sound like somebody kick their foot into a sack of grain. Frank bounce up quick, got some blood run from his mouth and nose. He stomp in a circle, put a whole lot of curses on Allen Decker.

"You gonna get a forest fire in your stomach," he say. "Your balls gonna rot off, make you smell like a skunk while they doing it. We gonna tie you down and put ants up your nose."

Decker ripple up his big muscles and gonna go for Frank again, but Miss Cartwright and Mr. Goldfinch don't let him. They talk about how they gonna have to make that movie and how Culture Canada can afford a new car. Finally they go away, Chief Tom drive all six of them in his little white sport car. Them Italians mens don't speak no English and only Mr. Goldfinch can talk to or understand them.

Next day they is back early though, take photo pictures of everything in sight.

"They would like to photograph some of your ceremonial dances," Mr. Goldfinch tell us. Then he explain that the Italian people is come all the way to Canada to photograph some fierce Indians like they read about in old-time books.

"How about a chicken dance?" we say. "Mrs. Chief Tom

Crow-eye do a mighty fine one."

"Okay," they say, and off we go to see Mrs. Chief Tom. Goldfinch be the only one friendly today. Miss Cartwright hang on to the arm of Allen Decker and he scowl mean at everybody. Miss Cartwright act like she ain't enjoy herself except once in a while she catch the eye of Frank Fence-post and smile kind of nice.

Rufus Firstrider play the drum and Mrs. Chief Tom do her dance. It is the saddest chicken dance this side of the cross and the Italian men after a while start take pictures of each other taking pictures.

After that we let them photograph us guys load Mad Etta in the back of Louis Coyote's pickup truck. We use the door from One-wound's outhouse for a ramp and a couple of us guys push and a couple pull to get her up there.

The stuff we show them don't excite them very much. Decker kick his boots at the dirt. Goldfinch wave his arms a lot and talk to the Italians who wave their arms a lot and yell at Goldfinch.

Us guys is busy trying to figure a way to get even on Decker for punch Frank's nose. We check around the motel in Wetaskiwin last night and find that Decker and Miss Cartwright sleep in the same room. If we don't be careful that could make for more trouble, cause Miss Cartwright, "Call me Marcia," she say, is all the time pull Frank off to one side say she want to practise up on her Cree speaking. Ain't too hard though for us to see what she really want to practise up on. We look at Decker stand around big as a mountain and figure that if he get mad enough to hit cause we wrecked somebody else's car . . . what would he do if he find out an Indian mess with his woman?

Frank teach Miss Cartwright some real dirty words, tell her they be things like, "How are you?" and "Have a nice day." We can hardly wait for her to try them out on Chief Tom who don't like to speak Cree no more anyway. We bust up laughing two or three times when we think about that.

Next day we tell them we have a real treat. We put some red spray paint on Rufus Firstrider and tell them he gonna do the wounded coyote dance. Rufus he have a hard time to walk without falling down so it be a pretty boring dance. After it over there is a big palaver and a couple of the Italians slap their hands on their mouths and make what they think is Indian dance noises to demonstrate for us what it is they want to see.

Goldfinch tell us that the Italians figure we ain't near as fierce as we supposed to be. He tell us that over in Italy all they know about Indians is what been wrote by this James Fenimore Cooper fellow. Everybody look blank when he say that. Guess I the only one who know of James Fenimore Cooper. Mr. Nichols say if I going to write down stories then I got to read a lot and he get for me from the library, *The Deerslayer*, *The Chain-bearer*, and a couple of other books so I can see how white men write about the Indian. Mr. Nichols say this Cooper fellow is mainly full of shit, but that people all over believe that us Indians still go around take scap and rape white women like Mr. Cooper's Indians did.

"If that what they want to see, we do it," I say. "For $200 we sort of make up a play. We pretend to be fierce and scary, take up a scalp or two, and rape us a white woman if we can find one."

Goldfinch explain all this to the Italians and he stomp in a circle and pound on his chest while he do it. They all nod their heads up and down and whir their cameras a lot.

"When?" says Goldfinch.

"Tomorrow," we say.

"You're not going to pay these thieving buggers?" says Decker.

"Shhh," say Miss Cartwright to him.

"Tomorrow, if we can find a white woman to rape or pretend to . . ."

"I've done some acting," say Miss Cartwright.

"The hell you will," say Decker.

"Oh Allen, it's only pretend," she says.

"He can be in the play too," say Frank. "We dress him up like a cowboy and take his scalp." When Frank say this he make sure he is far enough away from Decker that he don't get his nose bashed again.

"Hey," say Goldfinch, these guys want to know what a cowboy looks like. They say you Indians are all dressed up in denim like cowboys supposed to be. They want to know if cowboys dress up like Indians?"

We never thought of that before and can't come up with any answer for them.

That evening a bunch of us sit around Mad Etta's cabin try to figure out what kind of a play we put on and also how to get even on Allen Decker.

"When it come to the play we really kill him by accident," suggest Rufus Firstrider, and for his share of the $200 he offer to let us use his girlfriend, Winnie Bear, who be white, for the lady to get raped.

"Mad Etta maybe could help if you was to ask her," say Etta, smile from way down inside her fat face where her eyes be hidden.

"How?" we say.

"Etta got some stuff here," she say, and go get a medicine bag been hanging from her stove pipe. Inside is crow feathers wrapped around something be green and slimy and look like it been squeezed out of a boil.

"Here's what you do," she say to us and tell us her plan.

Later on, Frank and me drive down to Hobbema to the pay telephone and call the motel in Wetaskiwin.

"Miss Cartwright, this here's Frank Fence-post. I was figuring maybe we should practise up for that there rape scene . . ." and he invite her up to the reserve in an hour, be sure she come alone.

Back at Mad Etta's she point at the medicine bag. "Bad medicine come from Donald Bobtail the time he got messed up with that girl in Edmonton. Never know when you need something like that . . ."

"Kind of a culture?" I say.

"Huh?" say Etta and Frank together. "Silas reads too many books," Etta says.

"How you keep stuff like that growing and alive?" ask

Frank.

"Etta take a crow, cut out the bones, wrap what left around the medicine what been mix with cow brains. Keep forever long as it warm." Then Etta laugh and laugh, shaking on her tree-trunk chair, and I know that part of the reason she laugh is that there is not much truth in what she told Frank.

"You make sure Frank he don't tough none of our Indian girls before he come back to see me," Etta say to me, "or we have us a whole lot of troubles," and she laugh again. "Now you get on out of here, Silas. I got business with Frank."

"He be my friend and I supposed to be your assistant. How come I can't stay?"

"Out," she say, and wave her beefy big arm at the door.

I go but I stop right outside.

Etta chuckle from way down inside, sound like a trail bike backfiring. I hear her get up from her chair.

"Soon as you done what we talked about you come back here and I give you this medicine to make you better again. It taste a little like gasoline but then I always hear you brag about how tough you is . . ." I can hear Etta's big feet make the cabin floor creak.

"Okay, now drop your pant," she say to Frank.

"Do I got to?"

"Hey, Etta was there when you was born. She seen you naked before . . ." I hear Frank's belt buckle snap. "Besides Etta's your medicine man. This here is strict business . . . Wow! You got a buffalo back in your family someplace? You should be twenty years older or I should be twenty year younger, cause Etta sure don't mind have a good whack at what you got in your pants there," and her and Frank have a good laugh, but they is different kinds of laughs. Frank's is happy, as if he just killed something with his bare hands. Etta's is wishful.

I wait for Miss Cartwright and when she get to the reserve I take her into Frank's cabin.

"Where is everybody?" she say.

"He's around," I tell her. Then I take the soft laces from my moccasins and tie her wrists, one to each outside bar at the top of the bed.

"How come?" she say, but I can tell she don't mind the idea.

"If you gonna be raped you got to pretend to be helpless. This just make it easy for you."

As I go out the door Frank jump up from the trees. He got a headband hold back his long hair, blue paint on his cheeks, no shirt and he wipe some red and green paint on his chest.

He jump up into the doorway and I hear Miss Cartwright kind of gasp but not loud enough so's anybody else would hear.

I close the door, but before I go, I take one little peek in the window at Frank as he do a little war dance. I go away when I see him undo his belt, the one with the green buckle say Lethbridge Pale Ale on it.

dreams

"Hey, Silas," Frank Fence-post says to me, "ain't that your old man?" And he point across the bar of the New Edmonton Hotel to where a guy is stand beside a table talking to some people. The guy got his back turned toward us but I can tell it is my father and my belly get all of a sudden tight like maybe I been holding my breath a long time.

It be a Saturday night and me and Frank borrowed Louis Coyote's pickup truck and drove up here to Edmonton with our girlfriends. Sadie One-wound is mine. Connie Bigcharles is his. Me and Sadie went and got a room at the Alberta Hotel, seven dollars for the night and the room got a sink of its own and a bathroom right down the hall with a tub and everything. It only got a single bed though which ain't so great cause we was gonna sneak Frank and Connie up the fire-escape. But Frank he been sleep on the floor all his life so I guess one more night won't make no difference.

I wondered a lot of times about how I feel if I saw Papa again. I ain't seen him for a long time, since I was maybe ten or eleven. Paul Ermineskin, my father, be what everybody say is a really bad bastard. When he lived with us he drink a lot and he get mean when he drink. But Papa he weren't even a very nice man when he was sober. He liked none of us kids and he don't care so much for Ma either. Always make me wonder why a man who feel like that make himself such a big family.

He stand and talk at that table for quite a while, then he move off to another one. He got kind of a scuffling walk, like a lame dog.

"You gonna kill him or what?" Frank says, and he jump up and down a little, and Connie Bigcharles squeeze his arm and look over at me with really big eyes.

Me and Frank been friends all our lives and I've said to him sometimes that I'd like to kill my old man, if I ever seen him again, for all the bad things he done to my mother and us kids.

My father don't stay long at the next table before he move on. I figure what he doing is try to bum change or get to drink a free beer. He stop at the table behind us and I get to hear some of what is said.

Frank got with him a five-inch hunting knife and he take it out and lay it on the table.

Sadie don't say nothing but she look worried at me and I see she just light up a cigarette even though she got one going.

Papa knows the people at the table behind.

"Harvey, how you doing?" he says.

"What you want?"

"Just passing the time. You borrow me a cigarette?"

The guy, Harvey, is about to give Papa a cigarette but Harvey's woman, a thin lady with high cheekbones, look like an Athabasca, say, "Don't give him nothing. He's a mooch. You give once you never get rid of him."

Harvey put his cigarettes away in his shirt pocket.

44

"Bitch!" Papa say to the woman. Then he mumble some to himself and start to move away. Then all of a sudden he turn back to the table and start to call them both the most awful names he know. Names I heard him use on us and Ma when I been little.

Harvey he stand up and he be a lot bigger and taller than Papa. It seem funny to look at Papa now and see that he is pretty small and short. He always seem like kind of a giant to me before. I must be four or five inches taller than him and a lot stronger built. Him and Harvey argue for a minute and the woman be busy cursing him out good. Then Papa slap over a couple of beers, the glasses break and they go all over the woman. Harvey hits Papa with a pretty good right hand, make him stagger back and fall hard. This kind of surprise me too cause they still tell around the reserve about how Papa was about the best fist fighter there was. Harvey goes after him in case he gonna get up and fight some more but Papa just lie there while Harvey give him a couple of kicks to the shoulders and then walk back to his table where the woman still cursing and wipe beer off her clothes.

"You gonna go help him, Silas?" Sadie say to me.

"No way," say Frank, shaking his head.

I sure feel funny. My hands are kind of shake even though I don't want them to. For the first minute it make me feel some good that Papa get back some of his own. I hardly know that I'm doing it but I get up from the table and go over and help Papa get up to his feet. I take him to a table for two over by the wall.

When I'm holding his arm it feel all skinny, like a bird feel under its feathers. I signal the waiter for another beer. He set two in front of me but says, "We don't serve this guy in here. He's a troublemaker."

"It be okay this time," I say. "This here's my Papa."

After I say this is the first time that Papa look at me. He smile a little.

"By God," he say, "Silas, I don't know if I'd of knowed you or not."

Neither of us know for sure what to do so we shake hands across the table. His is dry as a handful of brown leaves. He got some blood trickle down off the side of his face but he don't seem to notice none. His eyes seem pretty small but in the middle of them it look like he got shiny nails pointing out.

"If I had some money, Silas, I'd buy you a beer."

"It's okay," I say. We talk for a while. I point out Sadie to him and she give us a little wave with her hand. I see that Papa ain't so drunk as I thought but that it just seem like he is awful tired. He got a bad cough and it seem to me that his mind wander sometimes.

"I never seen the baby," he say.

"Ma named her Delores. She is start third grade this fall. Got most of her front teeth out. She look like a little pumpkin when she laugh."

"Illianna used to be like that. I used to shake Illianna on my knee. She was a pretty little girl used to hug my neck and kiss me."

Then he kind of shake his head. "I heard she got married."

"She live in Calgary. You got a grandson called Bobby." I don't know if he know that Illianna married with a white man but I sure ain't gonna mention it if he ain't.

"By God, I'm a grandfather. I don't feel no different."

Papa's hair is some longer than I remember. It used to be short, stiff and sharp as snare wire, and black. There be spots of grey in it now, kind of like frost on winter grass. I trying to figure how old Papa is and guess that he can't be no more than 45.

"If I had some money, Silas, I'd buy you a beer. Celebrate being a grandfather." He smile at me when he say that and I can see that in a lot of ways I look like him. "You borrow me a cigarette?"

I put a couple in my shirt pocket and push the pack over to him.

"I remember when I was a young guy like you. Used to have some good times: go to the dances at Blue Quills or over to Bittern Lake Hall on Saturday night. Lots of the young girls used to go after me in them days. I remember one girl with a yellow scarf in her hair . . . I don't think it was your ma. I was gonna do a lot of things in them days . . . own my own place, and something special that I used to dream about . . ."

He stop and cough a long time. Then he take a drink of his beer. "Then I got married to your ma. Suzie was a pretty girl. Good Catholic too, went to the convent school. A man's got to have him a woman. I see you got yourself one. Not near as pretty as your Ma. Suzie used to look at me like that once. Bet you never figured that, huh? The way we used to fight." We sit silent for quite a while before he speak again.

"You don't think much of me, huh, Silas?"

I don't know what to say so I don't say nothing. I just order us up some more beer.

"Don't think I don't feel bad about what I done. It just that I don't know how to be no different. I met Bertha Calf-robe one time, over to the Cecil Hotel. She run off to the city and left Gus with eight or ten kids. 'Well, Paul Ermineskin,' she say to me, 'guess you an me we pull an even team. We both bad buggers that nobody want around.' So we get drunk together and we get a gallon of wine and a room. And when we real drunk we cry for our kids that we run away from. But we know deep down that we wouldn't go back even if we could, neither of us. And that make us more sad, so we drink until we pass out, and we sleep until the manager come round and kick us out the next day.

"You were a good boy, Silas. I remember one time we went to Wetaskiwin. I got good and drunk and you drove the team all the way home by yourself. You make me real proud that time."

"You boxed my ears for driving so rough on the road up to the reserve that it wake you up."

He shake his head some. "I'm . . . sorry I done that. If I had some money I'd buy you a beer, Silas."

We sit quiet for a while. Papa's eyes kind of close and I figure maybe he gonna sleep some.

"You like to get something to eat, Papa? We could go to

a café . . ."

"Don't remember when I ate last," he mumble. "I stay over to the Sally Ann or else sleep out . . . but the nights getting pretty cold."

I picture Papa sleep in doorways the way I seen Indian men around the downtown.

I think real fast try to figure what I could do for Papa. I could never bring him home, but maybe a room in Wetaskiwin near the Tech School where I could keep an eye on him.

"You do anything, Silas?"

"Work, you mean?"

"Yeah."

"I wonder if I should tell him that I write down stories. I decide not to. "I take a course that the Government offers, learn how to fix big tractors and stuff."

"Indians can do that now?"

"Sure, the Great White Father let us do lots of things."

"Except what I wanted."

"What was that?"

"Suzie never old you about it? You know, maybe I never told her. Guess maybe I just keep it to myself. Maybe I shouldn't tell you in case you laugh."

"I don't laugh at you, Papa. I promise."

"I wanted to be an auction man."

"An auctioneer?"

"I know. I talk, people say, like I got a mouthful of rocks. But when I was a boy I used to hang around the auction barn up to Wetaskiwin, listen to them sell off cattle. When the auction man be talking fast it be like the chants that the dancers do when we have ceremonies on the reserve, or like the sounds that medicine men make over sick people. When I hear it I get all shaky inside and all excited too. I figure that instead of really do the auction singing that I get a job around there so I could be close and maybe someday learn . . . but the guys there don't want no Indians around. They say I steal from them. That be why I did later on. I got put in jail for that.

48

"Sometime here in the city I go over and just hang around the crowd at O'Hara Auctions. Pat O'Hara is a pretty good man, used to let me work a day now and then unload trucks, but I don't think I could do that no more. I'm getting pretty tired these days."

I sure would like to do something for Papa. Still, I remember the bad times too. Times when we kids hid under the bed so he couldn't get at us. Time he left for good he broke up all the dishes in the house, throwed them through the kitchen window, them that he didn't smash on the floor or the stove.

Ma was big with her baby, like she was holding a wash tub in front of her. She stood in the corner with a butcher knife and she hold it with both hands with the point on her belly and say if he come after her she ain't gonna kill him she gonna kill herself. That kind of slow him down some and he finally go away. Me and Joseph and Illianna we watch it all from under the bed.

I wonder if Papa remember that?

"Papa," I say, "I sorry that you couldn't be an auction man, but . . ."

And then Frank is come to our table. I introduce him to Papa.

"Fence-post," Papa say, "you be Tom Fence-post's boy. I'd of never knew you since you grew up."

"Yeah," say Frank. "Tom was my old man."

"He was a son of a bitch," Papa say real loud. "Claimed I stole a set of harness one time. I'd fix that bastard good if he was here," and he stand up and make a fist in Frank's face.

Frank reach for the knife in his belt and I sure glad that he left it over on our table.

"Papa," I say, "Tom Fence-post been dead for four or five years now."

"He's still a son of a bitch."

I step between Papa and Frank to keep Frank from hitting him. Papa's sharp little eyes glare at me.

"Sit down, Papa," I say to him. He draw back his hand at me but before he can do anything I give him a good shove on his chest that land him right back in his chair. God, but I sure hope he stay there and I sure breathe some easier when he does. I steer Frank away from the table and go back and sit down.

"I wish you hadn't done that," I say to Papa. "I start to feel there like we was a son and a father."

He look over at me and I can see his eyes have quieted down some.

"I didn't steal that harness."

"I believe you, Papa."

"Good. If I had some money, Silas, I'd buy you a beer."

"When you told me your dream there Papa, it make me real sad that you weren't ever able to get what you want, but it make me happy that you tell your dream to me. I want to tell you what I do, Papa. I write down stories. Mr. Nichols, the counselor at the Tech School, he fix up my spellings and get the secretary to type up my stories. I had some printed in magazines, Papa. And someday maybe I get me a whole book printed. Ain't that good, Papa? If you come visit me I show them to you to read."

I don't know what I expect but as I look across I can see Papa's eyes get sharp again.

"School be the white man's way of making you white. I never went hardly at all myself, and I don't send Illianna or you to school until they come round and say they put me in jail if I don't."

"People only get white as they want to be, Papa. Me and Sadie . . ."

"Never thought I'd have me a white man for a son!" Then he call me a bad name.

"Papa, I thought you'd be happy that some of my dream happening . . ."

"White man," he spit at me, and he start to get up again. "You want to fight me, white man? I can still whip you like I done when you was little . . ."

We standing in front of each other. I let him hit at me and it bounce off my shoulder. Before he can make no more trouble I give him a good hard push back into his chair and then I walk back to my table. We sit for another half hour or so and I keep sneak looks over at Papa who be kind of passed out. He is lean back with his legs stretched out in front of him. His left arm it hang at his side, limp like maybe it broken. In his right he got a cigarette burn down awful close to his fingers.

I go to the bar and buy him a box of beer: I check my wallet and see that I ain't got so much money, but I take my last ten-dollar bill and get the bartender to break it into ones so the cab driver won't rip off my Papa when it come time to pay.

"Come on, Papa," I say, and he look up surprised and like he don't know me. Frank and me help him outside and into a taxi. I put the key to our room in his shirt pocket and tell the driver where to take him.

"Jesus Christ, Silas," Frank he say to me, "I know he's your old man, but after all he done to you how come you still be nice to him? He be mine I'd of probably killed him."

"I understand him," I say.

"I'd sure never forgive a bastard like him. All your life he never done you nothing but dirt."

"Understand ain't exactly the same as forgive," I say.

"You give away our hotel room too," Frank say, but I hardly hear him, cause I'm thinking about the time Papa left home for good. Since the dishes was all broke, I went around to where different people spread their garbage and gather up some tin cans. I got a pair of snips from Mrs. Louis Coyote and cut the cans down so we could use some for cups, some for bowls, and some for plates, but the little kids cut their fingers and mouths on the sharp edges, so I had to go borrow a pair of pliers and bend the edges over.

"Understand ain't nowhere like forgive at all," I say as we sit back down with the girls.

Frank just pick his knife back up off the table.

john cat

The bar have so many farmer customers that cow manure be the first thing you can smell when you walk in. It be a dark place, in a town I forget the name of, with no windows except for some glass blocks up high, that you can't see through. Only hold 25 or so people and tonight not even half the tables is full.

Me and my friend Frank Fence-post shake the snow off our boots. We only have to walk about half a block from where we parked the truck, but it enough to make us pretty cold. The gravel road we drove in on be kind of pearly white, and even with rocks in the back of the half-ton for weight, it still skid some on us.

We passing through the Peace River country on our way to a lumber camp supposed to have jobs for us, and stop for a beer at this little farm town.

"How far until we get to Keg River?" I ask the waiter, but he just plunk down a couple of beers and pretend he don't hear me.

The table tops are $\frac{3}{4}''$ plywood and covered with cigarette burns. There is a table of six or seven farmers, fat men in bib overalls and mackinaws. A couple of old men sit alone at separate tables, and over behind the farmers is a drunk Indian.

Ain't hard to tell he's drunk. He is laying at his table with his legs out front in funny positions, like the legs of a half-opened-up folding table. His head roll around on his neck like it held there by a loose spring. He got half a beer on his table and a cigarette in his hand that burn right down to his finger.

One of the farmers tell a joke and they all laugh loud, sound like two or three tractors start up at once. This wake up the Indian and he stand to his feet and stagger some. He pick up his glass and walk on his rubber legs toward the farmers.

That Indian be stupid drunk. He walk up to the table of farmers, his face all twist out of shape like it be under a couple of inches of muddy water. He have his mouth open like he want to say something, though nothing come out but a kind of half laugh. His tongue roll around in the corner of his mouth and some spit run down his chin.

"Oh Jesus! Is he back again?" say a farmer.

As the Indian weave toward them he raise his glass up in the air, I think just for balance himself, but a big farmer figure the Indian gonna hit him, so he stand up and paste him a good one to the chin. The Indian drop like a sack of potatoes when you empty it. His glass break and he lay there on the snow-dirty floor in the beer and broke glass.

He groan some and make a choking noise.

"Give me a hand with him, Charlie," one farmer say to another. "We don't want him to barf in here," and they take an arm each and drag the Indian along on his back over to the door and throw him outside. A cloud of steam come in as the Indian go out. The farmers clump back to their table.

As they go by they look at us like they dare us to say that they done the wrong thing.

We finish up our beer and clear on out of there. Outside, the Indian lay on his stomach in the snow. He got on just a red and blue flannel shirt, jeans and worn-out work boots with one sole loose.

I turn him over and see that he is one scrawny Indian, light as if he made out of straw. The wind be cold as hell and the exhaust from a car angle-parked at the curb whip around the bumper and break up in pieces.

Frank and me look at each other.

"He freeze if we leave him," I say. Frank nods.

I take the shoulders, Frank take the feet and we haul him to the truck. First thing he do is throw up all over: the dash, the seat, the floor.

We sit for a minute wonder what we gonna do.

"By morning at least the smell be froze up some," say Frank. "Boy, it stink a dog off a gut wagon." That be a saying our medicine lady Mad Etta use whenever she smell something bad.

Just then RCMP car pull up behind the truck, its red light twirl round and round, bounce off store windows on both side of the road like a volleyball.

An RCMP guy come to each door of the truck. Biggest cops I ever seen, wear fur hats and buffalo-skin coats.

"They must feed on Indians to grow that big," say Frank as we get out.

They put us up against the truck and search us for knives and dope. They stick their heads inside the truck, screw up their faces at the smell, decide not to search in there no more.

The one on my side make me get out Louis Coyote's registration papers and insurance, and my driver's licence. He sure surprised that I got all three.

"You guys been drinking so I don't want you to move this truck until morning," say the RCMP guy on my side. He got a long brown moustache and his breath steam up his collar, moustache and eyebrows.

"We don't be drink with this guy, we just pick him off the street," say Frank, point to the Indian laying over sideways on the seat. "Me and Silas have only one beer each. You ask the guy inside the hotel."

"I said you been drinking," say the cop on my side, and drive his elbow about halfway through my back, I guess cause Frank be too far away for him to hit. The papers for the truck fall out of my hand and that cop kick them under the truck.

"If that truck moves before morning you're gonna be a couple of sorry bucks. Clear?"

"Clear," we say. I have to crawl on my belly in the snow to get back the papers.

We head down for the hotel again. This time we go around to the lobby part, leave the Indian on the step and go inside.

"You rent us a room, mister?" I say to the guy behind the desk.

"You being smart?" he say back at me.

"No, Sir," I say.

I sure don't want no trouble from anybody else tonight. It could be maybe 50 miles to the next town.

"Goddamn Human Resources says we've got to rent to Indians," the clerk say. "Tear the shit out of my rooms you buggers do."

"We try to be careful," I tell him as he sign me and Frank up.

"We got another guy out on the step there," say Frank. "One who don't feel so good."

"I shoulda known," say the clerk. "Let's have a look at him."

We bring in the Indian, lay him on the floor in front of the desk.

"Where'd you get him? He's been bumming around town the last few days. You relatives?"

"We sort of brothers," I lie.

"What's his name?"

"We don't know."

"Well, look in his clothes. Can't register him if he don't have a name."

I dig in the back pocket of his jeans and find a slip of paper from the Unemployment, say his name be John Cat.

"That'll be two dollars extra," say the clerk, "and if he pukes you got to clean it up."

"We know," we say.

The room smell like it been closed up for a long time. It got a bed with a dark green spread, a dresser, a little table and a silver-painted radiator that make noises like somebody banging on it with a wrench. Everything in the room, even the dark-brown linoleum, got cigarette burns on it.

We first hold our Indian over the sink see if he want to puke some more, and when he don't we lay him crossways on the bottom of the bed. He mumble some and swing his arms at me and Frank while we do it. John Cat have that rotten sock smell about him like a people that ain't washed himself for a long time.

We try to decide what to do with him, can't think of nothing, so we leave him across the bed there. Me and Frank scrunch up our legs and get under the covers with our clothes on.

"Who the hell are you guys?" be the first words John Cat say to us in the morning.

"You was sleeping on the street," say Frank. "We don't figure you look good froze stiff so we bring you in."

John Cat be probably around 30 or so. He got a long, thin face, hair that stick out all ways and look like it been cut by himself. You can hardly tell if he got any lips and his mouth be full of yellow teeth look like they climbing over each other.

"I was sure good and drunk last I remember," he say.

We buy him and us breakfast in the Chinese café next to the hotel. When we tell him we headed up Keg River way he ask to come along. Say he know the way to where we going and can give directions. This here country be one long way, must be 300 mile or more, from where Frank and me come from.

John Cat tell us he work in a camp around Keg River until a month or so ago. "Got my pay and hitched down to Grande Prairie for a two-week toot. Had a good one too," he say and grin his yellow teeth at us.

When we leave town it be snowing some, lazy flakes that hang in the air like a swarm of white flies. Twenty mile or so down the road, when we be on a long straight stretch with just snow banks on each side, I see the brake lights flash on a car travelling way ahead of us. That car swerve sharp, then speed up and be gone.

When we get to the spot where the car swerve I see a body lay up against the snowbank. I brake the truck to a stop.

"What you doing?" say John Cat.

"There's a man beside the road."

"Shouldn't stop," he say, but me and Frank already out of the truck.

The man be a boy, fourteen or so and Indian. He already got snowflakes settle in his hair. There be blood run from his mouth and his breath make choke sounds like his throat be full of something. I took, one time, this here St. John the Ambulance Man Course, at the Wetaskiwin Community Hall. And from what I remember about first aid, I know we sure shouldn't move this guy.

I look all around but there ain't nothing but scrub tamarack and muskeg as far as I can see. The wind seem to be blow harder.

"Let's get out of here you guys," John Cat yell from the window of the truck.

"Boy's hurt," Frank yell back.

"Don't matter. RCMP come along, they blame you for hit him. We all go to jail or worse."

"We got to get help," I say.

"You don't know this country. RCMP kill Indians that don't say 'Yes, Sir,' loud enough. Trust me and go," John Cat insist.

I can feel my ribs hurt where that big constable hit me last night.

Frank and me talk for a while. We figure if nobody come by soon that him and John Cat will stay with the body while I drive to the next town to call an ambulance.

After ten minutes or so a pickup truck come out of the snow from behind us. I run out in the road and flag him down. If he could of got around me he would of, but finally he stop.

"What's wrong?" He a white man, 45 maybe, got a lined face like he work outside.

"Boy been hurt bad."

"You hit him?"

"No. We stopped. How far to the next town?"

"Twenty miles."

"You going there?"

"Yeah."

"The boy hurt too bad for us to move. You call an ambulance. We stay with the body."

"Sure," say the guy, but he is sure in one rush to get out of there. I figure it be more to get away from us than for hurry to call the ambulance.

"He'll send the police," say John Cat. "You don't understand this country. They lock us all up. I seen it before."

"Be quiet," I tell him.

"Indians here is wrong even if they right. RCMP don't care about that Indian on the road. They just got to blame somebody for hit him and it be us."

Another car come along. He just beep his horn loud and make me jump out of the way. Same thing happen with a car and a four-ton truck come from the other direction.

By now the boy pulled his legs most up to his face and his breath come in little short puffs, like a dog panting. We ain't got blankets or nothing.

Frank and me look him over and decide that there ain't time for me to go for help and that we got to take the chance and load him up in the truck, drive for a hospital.

While we go back to the body John Cat move over behind the truck wheel and pull the truck up beside us.

"What are you doing?" I say. I try to get in the truck but

he locked both doors and got his window open only a little bit.

"I driving out of here," he say. "You can stay and freeez or come along."

"The boy need help. We can't leave him."

"I do this for your own good," John Cat say. "Make up your mind quick."

I keep try the door. John Cat move the truck ahead slow and signal us to get in the back. I figure quick that all three of us probably freeze if we stay out here. John Cat keeps pull the truck away. All I have time to do is take off my jacket and lay it over the boy beside the road.

We freeze in the back until the next town. John Cat stop the truck at a service station and step out.

"You guys can beat on me if you want," he say. "What I done keep us all out of jail. Maybe for a long time."

"It weren't right," I say.

"According to you," say John Cat. "You guys been to school. White man learn you some of his ways. You got something to hide behind. I just a bush Indian do what he have to do to stay alive."

"It still wasn't right to leave him."

"What's right depend on where you at. Where you come from might be different."

Maybe John Cat is right. I have to think on it.

Just maybe. Across from the service station is a school house. I walk across and talk to an Indian kid about ten. I ask if for a dollar he'll take a message to the mounties. I tell him, if they ask, it was a white man in a big car give him the dollar.

Up the road aways the truck break down and it take us most of the day to get it wired together again. It snow so heavy we can hardly see where the road is. I pull off onto a rest area and we decide to sleep for a while. We got enough gas to last until morning and then some.

When we wake up the sunshine be sharp as pins on our eyes. Way down the road I see the blue light of a snow plow.

Me and Frank slept solid as lumber, only John Cat jump

up twice in the night, yell loud and throw his arms around.
Frank and me have to tell him where he is and that everything be all right.

the kidnapper

Hardest thing I know of to do is visit someone in a hospital. Even if it be someone you like, the stiffness of the hospital make it so you talk like strange people do in a bus depot.

Last fall, about September, my friend Old Joe Buffalo is have a stroke. I figure it is sure lucky that it happen to him while he was walk down the street in Wetaskiwin. If it been out at his cabin on his farm he would of been sure to die before anyone found him. Joe, near as I can figure be well over a hundred years old.

He been my friend since I was a boy. We done some secret things together and Joe teach me most of what I know about the old-time customs of our people. Joe he outlived three wives and his only daughter Ruth died a long time ago.

When Joe fall down sick, he just lay on the sidewalk for

a while until someone call the RCMP guys to come and get the drunk Indian off the street. RCMP put him in a cell but when he don't sober up in a few hours they take him to the hospital.

When we was all little kids at the reserve school, they bussed us up to Edmonton one time to walk around a dairy and see how milk made. What I remember best was how clean everything was. Everywhere was metal and bright light and it may of been clean, but it weren't friendly. Hospitals is like that.

Where they got Old Joe weren't really no hospital but is called the Sundance Retirement Home and is in Wetaskiwin not far from the grain elevators. It be a low flat building done up in a kind of peach-coloured stucco. Outside there be a totem pole carved by a guy used to live on our reserve. The halls is all covered in dark brown linoleum colour of wet sand. The whole place smell like the toilet in some of the beer parlours I been in. First time I go there I stand around shuffle my feet and my boots make tracks on that floor look like waffle irons. I seen them once make waffles at the Gold Nugget Café, but I never ate one. That sure be a funny thing for me to think about lookin at my feet, but I guess it be I nervous. Sure don't much like being in white people's places.

They don't much want to have Old Joe in that place either, but the Government say they got to since he ain't a treaty Indian. Joe bought his own farm across from the reserve and he live on it for maybe 80 years or so.

Big fat white lady with red hair look like that there Ronald McDonald fellow is take me down the hall to where they keep Old Joe Buffalo and sniff up her nose all the time like maybe I smell bad. She keep join her fingers together and then take them apart real fast.

The fat lady tell me that Old Joe can't talk and that he be in a pretty bad way. His room is so small that there don't be space for the both of us to stand up in there along with the bed and the dresser. The white lady pretty glad to leave quick. The walls is painted light green. There is a window

62

but it look out on another window that look back at us.

Soon as we alone, Old Joe he say to me, "I don't like for you to see me like this, Silas. They got me wearing a white man's dress."

Sure enough they have Old Joe in one of them white hospital dresses. He look tiny as a child way up there in that high hospital bed. His face be wrinkled and brown as the calfskin rattles Mad Etta, our medicine lady, keep in her cabin to make spells and things. He say that to me in Cree and his voice be like the sound of walking on dried leaves.

"Lady say you don't be able to speak."

"Only to them," and he make a little laugh like he clearing his throat.

It sure hard for us to think of things to say to each other. Joe tell me that he can hardly move his left arm and leg and that it seem like he forgot all the English he ever knowed. He doze off to sleep a couple of times and I pretty glad to go away. But Joe been my friend for a long time so I go see him every few days from then on.

"I try to will myself to die," he tell me one day. "But I guess my body be tougher than my head."

I sure feel bad for Joe and wish that I could do something nice for him. I tell him how I figure he be better before long and I come out to his place and help him lay out muskrat traps and stuff, but guess we both know it just be talk.

"Try never to get old, Silas," Joe say to me. "Young men like you figure old people used to being old but it ain't so."

That's what I thought all right. I figure you just accept get old cause everybody does it. That ain't the way it is for Joe though.

"Silas, I feel like maybe I been captured by an enemy tribe and their medicine man paint my face with wrinkles, dye my hair white and take away the strength from my arms and legs by cast some powerful spell. This here busted-up body is strange to me. Inside, I don't feel no different than I did as a young man."

"Kind of like you was kidnapped, huh?"

I never think about getting old in that way before. I glad

when Joe doze off to sleep and I can go.

One thing Joe sure miss is his pipe. He never smoke tobacco but wild grass and roots and stuff. People there at Sundance Retirement Home don't let him smoke his pipe cause it stink up the place too much. Joe tell me the Indian names for the sweet grass and leaves that he want and I get Mad Etta to help me pick them before it snow for good. I close up the door to Joe's room, open the window and me and Joe have us a good smoke until that nurse come along tell us we can't do that no more cause the smoke come out from under the door even though it closed.

"You know what I be like, Silas?" Joe say to me one day. "You know how apples drop off the trees in the fall but one or two stick to the tree and shrivel all up and hang on to the branch right into the middle of winter. That be me. Might be okay for apples, but they don't have to wear the white man's dress and go to the toilet in a tin dish."

Mad Etta come up to the hospital with me one day wear her medicine man outfit with fox tails down each sleeve of her five-flour-sack dress and she got on fur leggings and war paint. She be too big to get through the door to Joe's room but she do a little ceremony in the hall and scatter some pebbles around and sure scare hell out of that red-head nurse.

"I want to go back and visit my place one more time," Joe tell me. "You ask the white peoples if it be okay."

I ask the fuzzy-headed lady but she screw up her face and take me to see the manager guy, a Mr. Patterson who got a grey suit and face and a handshake like a piece of chamois.

He talk real loud to me cause I guess he figure Indians don't hear so good and explain like a teacher that Old Joe be way too sick to even move out of his bed.

When I tell Joe that he look at me with his eyes that still shine like a cat's do in the dark, make a little smile and say, "We show them who can get out of the bed or not."

For the next couple of days I look careful around the Sundance Retirement Home see where all the doors and stuff is. Then one night when it be about time for me to go,

I climb down and hide under Joe's bed. Real late in the night I get his clothes from the dresser and help him on with them. I wore my moccasins and me and Joe we go down the hall and that shiny linoleum might as well be muskeg moss for all the noise we make on it. We slip out the side door like not much more than shadows. The truck be parked a block or so away and I can see that Joe getting tired pretty quick so I scoop him up and walk down the street to the truck. He is light as my littlest sister.

"Bet I the oldest baby you ever have to carry around."

"Next time I bring a moss bag put you on my back like a papoose." We both have a good laugh together about that.

We drive down the highway in Louis Coyote's pickup truck. Snow be blow across the black road like waves of water. I take out of the glove box some of the roots and wild grass that old Joe like for his pipe. I fill his pipe up and light it for him.

I drive slow down the lane to his house on the farm, breaking trail all the way, cause I guess nobody been there since Old Joe been sick. I park with the lights shine on his cabin. It look awful small and there be snow drifted up against the door.

I start to get out of the truck but Old Joe stop me.

"I just want to have a look at it, Silas. I don't plan on going in." I feel my chest get tight. "You know that all along, don't you?"

"Yeah," I say. "I knew."

My face is doing things I don't want it to do.

"Which you figure is better for an old bugger like me, out here on my land or back there in the little box the white man keep me in?" And he do his little laugh again and open the truck door with his good hand.

We walk slow up the hill from his cabin and when we get to the top we stop and I help Old Joe sit down cross-legged. It cleared off some and the moon make everything kind of an icy blue colour, the Northern Lights run across the field like the shadows of dancers and seem sometimes to be almost close enough for touch.

I light up Joe's pipe for him and as I do I try to think of something good to say, but I can't. He just look straight ahead across the wheat fields where someplaces the stubble show a little through the snow. In the distance is some spruce trees and behind them the highway where once in a while the lights of a car go by.

I remember one time about Joe telling me what kind of clothes to wear on the trap line. "Look at your jeans," he say to me. "You get one inch of the cuffs wet and the water soak up most to your knee. Wear wool pants or buckskins then if you get wet you shake it right off, don't freeze off your leg for the wolves to eat." I told him I'd try to remember that.

slaves

"Gifts make slaves like whips make dogs," say Mad Etta our medicine lady as she tip up her bottle of Lethbridge Pale Ale, and in the light from the coal-oil lamp in her cabin her face shine kind of golden.

We was talking about Alma O'Connor, and Etta say what she say in Cree and it be kind of hard to make into English. And she say it in kind of a sharp voice like maybe I'm dumb to ask the question I did. All I said was, "Why do you figure Alma O'Connor acts the way she does?"

This summer I worked on a farm for a while. It was owned by an old farmer named John Tennant. He put an ad in the newspaper for somebody to fix up his fence. I think he was a Frenchman or something because he had an accent of some kind when he talked.

First time I go there he keep me talk in the front yard for

about four hours. John Tennant got a nose like a strawberry and grey hair the colour of snow that been walked in. His wife is dead, his kids growed up and away, and he used to work on the railroad when he was young. We agree that I'm gonna fix his fence for him for three dollars an hour.

When it come time to leave he say, "Look, young fellow, I take up your whole afternoon so I'm gonna pay you like you worked here" and he give me ten dollars. I figure that's awful good pay just for listen to an old man with a funny accent talk all afternoon.

"Where you ever gonna wear a dress like that to?" I say to Sadie as she climb into the pickup truck in O'Connor's front yard.

"When you get your book printed up maybe they put you on the television and I have to look good for you," and Sadie wrinkle up her nose at me and lean over to kiss my face. She holding on real careful to a cinnamon-coloured dress that made out of silk or something. It sure seem funny to me that those dresses of Alma O'Connor's fit my girlfriend Sadie One-wound like they was made for her. I always thought Alma was a lot bigger. She was seventeen when she get married and I was only twelve. A kid and a growed-up lady. Now I'm twenty and she's 25 and her dresses fit my girlfriend.

"You shouldn't let her give you stuff," I say as I reach over and touch the dress a little. It is cold and slippery as a snake and is covered with clear plastic, not the thin kind you get from a dry cleaner but the thick kind you buy in a store.

"She say she never wear it, Silas, so I might as well have it. She say everytime Mr. O'Connor go to Edmonton he bring her back something nice. She showed me her closet. It half as big as your cabin and it got I bet a hundred dresses in it, and fur coats and a piece of white fur that you wrap around your neck."

The cinnamon-coloured dress be about the same shade as Alma O'Connor, who used to be Alma Cryingvision before she got married.

Sadie's skin be dark as plowed ground and I bet she look

good in that dress, but where could she wear it? Anyway I like her better in jeans.

"It still don't seem right for you to take stuff like this that cost a lot, when she pays you too." Sadie's eyes darken up some.

"She got a dress red as a cardinal that she say I can have one day."

As we pull out of the yard onto the highway we pass Mr. Jim O'Connor's big Chrysler New Yorker coming in. He smile all over his face, wave his hand and beep the horn at us. Jim O'Connor always remind me of one of those real big puppies that jump up on you with their front paws.

He meet Alma Cryingvision when she come work on his people's farm during the wheat season. She help do the cooking for the threshing crews. The O'Connors be really rich farmers come from around a town called Kavanagh about fifteen mile north of the reserve on the main highway.

Alma's family name come about because long ago some Indian claim he saw the Virgin up at Bittern Lake. Claim she was kneel there in winter on the edge of the ice, all covered in thick white frost and crying ice tears. No-one but that one Indian ever see that vision so the church never do nothing about it, but guess Alma be some kind of a long distant relative of his.

Jim and Alma's wedding was a big deal. Not very often that a white man marry an Indian girl and everybody be happy about it. They have the wedding in the big Catholic church in Wetaskiwin. The church be all built of dark-coloured stone and it always seem like evening around close to it. O'Connors told Alma that she could invite as many friends as she want and I remember Ma getting this here fancy letter in the mail: a white card with a layer of tissue paper inside, and I had to read her what it said.

Instead of have the reception and dance at the Travelodge Motel in Wetaskwin like other rich peoples do, they have it on the reserve at Blue Quills Hall.

Us kids hung around the back of the dance hall and I remember how pretty Alma was. She be decked out in a white bride dress look like fog swirl up all around her. They done her hair up high on her head and she have what look like a halo of white up there. Her eyes flash black and she hold her back stiff as one of them shiny chrome coat racks you see in hotel lobbies. Jim O'Connor have a red flower on his suit. He have red hair, freckles like Rice Krispies, and a whole lot of wide white teeth when he smile. He smile enough for both of them that day.

The first day that I go to work for Mr. John Tennant the weather be soft as spring water. My body soak up the sun, the ground be spongy and the first crocus push up from the earth. I get there at ten in the morning the way I said I would. Mr. Tennant make me come in his house for coffee. It be a dark place with papers and clothes piled all over like any home where a man live alone. It smell of pipe tobacco and liniment of some kind.

Mr. Tennant he tell me all the same stuff he tell me the first time I was there, plus a couple of other stories about how he was in a train wreck and how one time he helped capture a crook who jumped off his train and hid in a culvert. I never even get close to the fence I supposed to fix and when it come evening Mr. Tennant pay me for six hours work and say he real glad I come around. I don't know what to make of it.

At the wedding I remember the Indian people talking about the marriage and how they all figure about the luckiest thing can happen to an Indian girl be to marry up with a rich white man. All but Mad Etta.

Morning of the wedding me and some kids carry Etta's tree-trunk chair from her cabin to Blue Quills Hall so she don't crack up regular chairs. She dress up for the wedding: have fox tails pinned down both sleeves of her five-floursack dress and deerskin leggings beaded with coloured porcupine quills.

"I don't like to see this happen," I hear Mad Etta say to my Ma. "Same as if she signing up to go to prison."

I don't remember what Ma said back to her, but I remember that I think Mad Etta be awful dumb, and I think that if I was a girl I'd sure try to marry me a rich white man.

After they been on a wedding trip all the way to California on an airplane, they don't live in with Jim O'Connor's people like you would expect. Instead, Jim he take over a couple of sections of wheatland over by Bittern Lake and he have built for him and Alma the biggest, longest and most expensive farm house around. Boy, you can see it every time you drive down the road from Wetaskiwin to Camrose. It got a bright blue roof and be finished in stone and stucco and look like 60–70 feet across the front and damn near as deep. There be a four-car garage and I hear that Jim buy new one of them Japanese compact cars for Alma's very own.

I don't have no reason to see them much for the next few years. They start a family right away. Like most Catholic peoples do, Alma have a baby each summer for three years. Boys, it say in the birth announcements of the Wetaskiwin Times.

Once in a while when some of the Indians from the reserve go to the Catholic church in Wetaskiwin they say they seen Alma and that she dressed like those ladies in the Eaton's Catalogue. Alma's folks get invited up to visit lots of times but they go only once. "I keep feel like I was going to make something dirty," Elias Cryingvision say one day, "I feel the same as the time I had to go to the courtroom in Wetaskiwin. I don't be able to breathe good until I get out of there."

It be a couple of years ago that Sadie start work for O'Connors. One day a notice show up on the bulletin board at Blue Quills Hall, ask for a girl to help out after school and do babysit on the weekends. I drove Sadie up to the O'Connor place. Sadie be really shy around white peoples and want me to come to the door with her but I don't. I notice that it is Jim O'Connor who answer the door.

While I wait I walk around the yard some. That whole house I bet is bigger than Blue Quills Dance Hall. Around the side be a big sandbox where two husky little Métis boys play. They tumble like puppies, fight some too and bang each other on the head with Tonka Toys.

Sadie get the job.

"I don't even get to see Mrs. O'Connor," she say. Mr. O'Connor figures it be good for her to have an Indian girl around. He say she been sick a lot lately.

I drive Sadie up there three days a week and once in a while on the weekend when O'Connors go off to a party or something. Sadie sure is excited to tell me all about the fancy house: how they got a refrigerator that make ice in your glass when you push a button, a microwave oven and a machine to make milkshakes just like in the Gold Nugget Café in Wetaskiwin. I think I might like to have that milkshake machine.

Bedelia Coyote say to me one day that Alma Cryingvision was just as shy around white people as my Sadie, and that the reason she marry Jim O'Connor is that she don't know how to say no to a rich white man. But then Bedelia don't think girls should get married, ever.

"You don't believe all the things she's got," Sadie say to me. "You never seen so much lipstick and perfume, and creams, and bath salts and oils in coloured bottles. And they got three bathrooms. Alma O'Connor got one all to herself that nobody else ever go into."

I think about the leaning-over outhouse behind Cryingvision's cabin. "Maybe you better start looking for a white man for yourself," I tell her, but Sadie don't even hear me.

"Look what she gave me," Sadie say, and reach in the pocket of her jean jacket and bring out some little bath salts wrapped in clear paper, look like gumdrops. She got too some eye-shadow stuff and three or four lipsticks.

"You spread that war paint stuff all over you and white guys be chasing you down the street in Wetaskiwin."

Sadie laugh some and put her head on my shoulder.

"I wonder why she don't like Mr. O'Connor more than she do? Boy, I sure never talk to a white man the way she talk to him, even if I was married to him."

"What does she do?"

"She try to make him feel bad. Tell him he don't give

her enough things . . . She ain't got room for many more things even in that big house."

Once in the winter when it be really cold, Mr. O'Connor come out to the truck as I pull up in front of the house.

"Why don't you come in, Silas," he say. "Sadie will be a few minutes late."

The living-room is big as a basketball court, all white carpet and dark brown furniture. The room be L-shaped and around the corner of the L Alma O'Connor sit at a polished wood table. The back wall of the house is all glass and you can look out over the wheat fields covered in snow all the way down to Bittern Lake.

Alma got in front of her a cup of coffee in a pretty little cup and saucer, and a long slippery orange ashtray look like it be made out of candy. She look at me kind of shy over the top of the cup. Then she tell her husband to get me a drink, only the way she say it be like she talking to somebody she don't like at all. She got on a dress green as spring poplar leaves and a scarf the same colour around her throat. She be so pretty she make my chest all tight.

That same winter Mrs. O'Connor learn to drive the car that been bought for her. At night she drive down to Weta-skiwin, people say they seen her sit alone at the Travelodge Cocktail Lounge, just sit stiff-backed with a bottle of Blue and a glass in front of her. But the white men don't leave her alone. They is always send over drinks and try to get friendly with her. Alma let them know she don't want nothing to do with them. She just sit quiet, get good and drunk and go home.

One night Alma drove her car into the ditch and the RCMP arrest her. She have to go to court and get fined $500, lose her driver's licence and get her name in the Wetaskiwin Times police court section.

After that Mr. O'Connor he take her every Tuesday up to Edmonton to see a doctor.

"He's one of them talk doctors. She say he sit way back in a chair with a light in front of him so she feel like she talking to the dark," Sadie tell me.

Folks from town tell the story that Alma O'Connor wandered off from the house in the late fall with only a white nightgown on and that they find her in the morning down by the lake all covered in frost just like the lady that her family named for. I only met people who heard about it, never anyone who seen it, though she was sick in bed with the pneumonia for a while in the fall.

After she lost her licence Jim O'Connor sometimes drive her up to Wetaskiwin in his big Chrysler New Yorker. She sit as close to her door as she is able to, and get out in front of the Travelodge without say good-bye. She have a few drinks at the cocktail lounge then she walk over to the Alice Hotel beer parlour. The Alice have mostly Indians and farmers for customers.

Some nights, about closing time, Mr. O'Connor come down to the bar try to get Alma to go home with him.

Once, he see me sitting at a table across the room and he walk over and say, "I think it's good for her to get out with other Indians . . . her own people . . . you know . . ." and his voice kind of trail off. He don't need to explain nothing to me and I wish he wouldn't.

That night Alma don't go with him and she raise up her voice to say awful things. Kind of things if she said to most any man I know she'd get her face punched. Mr. O'Connor have one hand on her shoulder. He finally take it off and go out the door, his own shoulders slumped over. I wonder if he know for sure that even though Alma be in an Indian bar she is always sit alone.

Third time I go to work for Mr. Tennant, I sneak to his place real quiet an hour before I supposed to be there. But I just get started tightening up some wire when he show up and keep talk to me for the whole day. I try to work but don't get nothing done. Mr. Tennant don't mind at all and he pay me off at the end of the day and give me an extra five dollars. For some reason I don't understand I be kind of mad at him for do that.

One day when I come to pick up Sadie, I see that Jim O'Connor's car ain't there, and soon as I stop the truck Sadie come to the door motion for me to come into the house. Alma O'Connor is sit at the long polished table with her tea cup and ashtray in front of her. She got her head down on her arms and is crying.

"She been do that all afternoon," say Sadie. "I don't know what to do with her."

Way off in the distance, like from across a field, I can hear the kids yelling and the television playing. Must be in the basement somewhere. Out the window the snow is deep and solid across the fields and I can see way off, a couple of bluey slashes that I know be the ice of Bittern Lake.

I figure maybe if I talk to her in Cree it make her feel a little bit better. I tell her how all us Indians figure she is about as lucky as she can get, have a happy kind of husband who don't knock her around. And how all the Indian girls wish they had a big house and car and all the fancy clothes that she got.

"Even if you just think of how nice and warm you are here, remember how your cabin have only a dirt floor and how there was only an oil-drum stove and how all the kids slept in one bed . . ."

Alma take a deep breath and kind of scream, but not quite, as she throw her tea cup against the wall. It smash and fall into the carpet, some of the orange flowers off the cup look like they growing in white grass.

I hear Mr. O'Connor's car pull up the drive.

"Would you like Mad Etta to come see you? Sometime she help people a lot sicker than you . . ." But Alma O'Connor just cry some more and don't answer me.

One night when a bunch of us going into the Alice Hotel bar, Mad Etta she waddle right up to Alma's table. Alma sit straight-backed, smoke her cigarette and drink beer.

"I hear you broke out of jail," Etta say. Her belly touch the edge of Alma's table but the rest of Etta be about three feet back.

Alma kind of shrink herself against the beer parlour wall. She say something cause I able to see her lips move, but she speak too quiet for me to hear. Etta, she don't say nothing, just turn around slow, like a big bear, and head over to where the manager got her two chairs wired together and braced with two-by-fours.

By now Sadie got a whole closet full of dresses and clothes that Alma give her. One day she come out of the house with a long face and a big brown paper bag. In it is that slippery-looking orange ashtray.

"All I said was that I sure thought it was pretty."

At my place we put it up on the shelf with the radio where my kid brothers and sisters can't break it.

"Silas, I don't want to go to work there no more." I put my arms around Sadie and she sniff into my shoulder.. "Worst thing is I don't understand why I don't want to."

"I know how you feel," I say. After three times I never go back to that Mr. Tennant's farm even though I get paid a lot for not do no work. But like Sadie, I can't find no words to explain why.

Alma Cryingvision O'Connor is sit most every night in the beer parlour of the Alice Hotel in Wetaskiwin. She be about 25 but her face look like for every day she live it get two days older. Not many people understand her. Even the Indians figure she should be home with her husband enjoy all the nice things he gives her.

"I understand," I want to go up to her and say, but I don't. We never did know each other very close. She's always been older than me.

the rattlesnake express

What happened was mostly done before I got to Edmonton. Dave Smallface from the Indian Friendship Centre is take away a girl named Lena from a guy called Melvin Rattle-snake.

I sure don't see why guys get so excited about something like that. Nobody ever takes one person away from another. If somebody go with a new person it be because they real ready to leave anyway and if it don't be this one it be somebody else pretty soon.

I be up here in Edmonton for take some course at Northern Alberta Institute of Technology for a month or so. Tech School at Wetaskiwin where I come from don't have all the courses they do in the big city.

Dave Smallface is a pretty big man among the Indians live in the downtown. He got a square face, deep-set eyes, and got strong arms that fill up his shirt. When he was on the reserve at Hobbema he used to box some and he was pretty good at it. He even grow him a beard and a moustache. Most of us Indians can't do that and the girls they sure go after Dave Smallface on account of that hair on his face. Me and my friend Frank Fence-post tried to grow beards one time. We shaved every day but all we got was about ten hairs each under our noses and nothing on the chin.

First day I be in town I go over to the Indian Friendship Centre in the evening. They got there a TV, some old, square red-and-green chairs and a sofa with holes in the arms. Basement have a ping-pong table that they made themselves but somebody busted all the balls and nobody ever remember to buy none. Government give money for rent the house and for pay Dave's wages. Dave he also do a pretty good business sell dope to his friends. He got marijuana, coloured pills, and some things he call windowpane acid and white lightning.

"What's this here white lightning?" I ask.

"Street acid," say Dave, "if it work right it make you feel like a white man, like a fucking sneak thief and a coward," and he laughs hard and cold.

Dave belong to the American Indian Movement and two or three other Red Power clubs. He all for kill off a few white men, if the chance ever come up.

"You live in the city, you live off the city, man," he say to me when I ask about if he ever get in trouble for sell dope. "It be just like running a trap line or skidding out logs, only a lot easier. You can get hurt do them things, too. Here your enemy is the man instead of the land."

It be just the day before that he move Lena into his room at the Centre. That night guys are make joke on him about this fellow they call the Express gonna sure be uptight about it.

When I been to the city before I seen the Express around the bars some nights. He got a long snake with its neck swoll up run all the way up the inside of his arm. His front teeth stick out some like he suck his thumb a lot when he be a baby. His whole name be Melvin Rattlesnake and he move fast and nervous, eyes never look at any one thing for long. I never understand for sure how he make his living but it seem to me that he pass information from one person to another. Somebody want to know where to score dope, he direct them. Somebody want to buy or sell some five-finger bargains, Melvin he arrange it. Don't never handle nothing himself, just spend his time walk from one bar to another along the drag. He call himself The Rattlesnake Express, guess cause he move around so fast, but most of them who know him just say, "Here come The Express," when they see him.

That evening whole bunch of us be sit around the Centre, smoke cigarettes, watch the black-and-white TV when Melvin Rattlesnake come in. He be skinny and got a wild animal kind of face. His long hair be wet some and combed back so he always look like he walking into a strong wind.

When Lena see him her face get a scared look on it and she slip out quick to her and Dave's room.

Dave sitting in a square chair with his leg up over the arm. He don't move at all just stare at Melvin and tap his cigarette ash on the floor.

"You take my woman," say Melvin.

Dave don't say nothing so Melvin repeat himself only louder.

"I ain't denying it," say Dave and blow smoke at the ceiling. "Suppose you want to fight me," he say like he really tired, and start to get slow out of his chair.

Melvin, his eyes make a quick trip around the room, though his feet don't go nowhere.

"You can have all the women you want. Why you have to take mine?" And I think I hear Melvin's voice kind of crack on his words.

I wonder about that too. Can't imagine what Dave Small-face see in that Lena girl. He can have about any woman he want, even the white ones hang around the Centre do what they call volunteer work, though mainly they like to go to

79

bed with Indian men and be what we call Indianstruck. Lena Smith is the girl's whole name. She be no more than sixteen, come from Slave Lake or someplace up there. She got a long, oval face, with pimples on her chin, sad eyes, and she hold her cigarette in a funny way so the smoke come up warm the palm of her hand. The Express pick her up off the street and they been together for a couple of months or so.

Clinton Wuttunee and a couple of other guys, most as big and tough as Dave, eye Melvin up and down and make like they going to get up. Dave he wave them back to their chairs. "Look, Express, I don't want no trouble from you. You know how women are. Go out and find yourself another one. There's lots around."

"For you maybe," say Melvin and his voice do break on them words and I can see from clear across the room that there be tears in his eyes. I guess maybe not so much from sorrow as from just be mad that he can't do nothing about what has happened to him. "You can have anybody you want," he say again. "You do this to me personal. I get you for it." Then he go out bang the door and we can hear his feet crunch the snow down the front steps of the house.

"We walk with you for a few days," say Clinton to Dave, "just in case he maybe hire some guys to beat you up or maybe come for you with a knife or something."

A few nights later we all sitting around a table at the York Hotel beer parlour, when in come The Express and walk right over to us.

"Miner down from Uranium City wants to score some acid," he say to Dave Smallface. "Room 203 at the New Ritz. I say I send you over with some white lightning." The New Ritz be a hotel just a couple of blocks away.

Melvin Rattlesnake disappear just as fast as he come.

"Ain't you afraid to take a deal from The Express like that?" I say. "Maybe he set you up for a bust."

"No way. Business is one thing, personal stuff is another. Besides, we be Indian first. Only white men turn in their brother to the man."

Clinton tell me too that Dave's had a couple of other

deals from The Express since their argument, and they turned out okay.

But not that time. When Dave Smallface don't come back to the bar by closing time we go over to the New Ritz and the clerk there say that there be cops all over early on, and that they hauled off an Indian guy to jail, from one of the upstairs rooms.

In the morning me and Geno Blanket go over to the Legal Aid office and one of the lawyer fellows phone the police and find out for us that they got Dave lock up for Traffic in LSD. They arrest him as he sell 250 tabs to an undercover cop. Bail be $2500.

The Express be around big as life that afternoon. "Hey, I know it look bad but you figure I stay around if I turned in Dave? I get bad information too, you know. Guy sure didn't look like a narc to me."

Clinton Wuttunee been up to see Dave and he say that even Dave don't figure that The Express turned him in. "Indians don't do that to one another," Clinton say Dave told him a few times.

There be a pretty good bank account of Government money for the Indian Friendship Centre. Dave he be able to sign cheques on it, so he arrange for make himself bail.

"Hell, I'd do the same for *them* if they was in trouble," he say with a laugh.

With Dave back on the street we make a little party at the York Hotel bar. We all laugh a lot and make jokes until Winston Fire-in-the-draw come by and change all that. Winston he been in jail for about two weeks, but has just been allowed to walk away from a charge of shoplift himself some five-finger bargains down to the Sears shopping centre. His legal aid lawyer make the police put him in a line-up and the lady store detective pick out the wrong Indian.

That make us laugh some until Winston say he wonder what The Express doing hang around the police station so much. Winston say his cell look out on the parking lot and he seen The Express two or three times last week slip down the alley and in a door mark for employee only.

"Look like you was wrong about The Express," say Clinton Wuttunee to Dave.

"Only goddamn white men do their brothers that way," yell Dave and throw a full glass of beer up against the wall of the bar.

The guys all figure we should do something but Dave just sit, lean his head on one hand and look at the table. Even Lena can't cheer him up none and he say under his breath quite a few times, "White man, fucking white man."

"Go home, woman," he say to Lena when she try to make him laugh, and the tone of his voice make her back away quick like a dog that been kicked.

After it get to be eight o'clock or so, Dave say, "Come with me," and he get up and all us guys go along with him. He lead us over to 97th Street and the Army & Navy Department Store. There Dave buy up a couple of gallons of paint and some brushes. Then we start down toward Jasper Avenue.

When we get there Dave look at me and say, "You get on out of here, Silas. You got no quarrel with The Express and we got none with you. We take our own weight if we get in bad with the man." And off go Dave Smallface, Clinton Wuttunee, Geno Blanket, Winston Fire-in-the-draw, and two or three other guys, some carry paint, some brushes.

The Express have himself a room up on the third floor of an old building across the street from the Alberta Hotel. No curtain on his window and I seen him move around up there as I walk down the street some evening.

I stand across the street there and watch the guys go in the building. The light be on in Melvin's room and I see him go answer the door and I see the shadows of the guys push into the room. Then somebody shut off the light. Nothing happen for a long time and I get pretty cold stand outside and figure it about time to go into the Alberta and have a beer. I look across Jasper Avenue watch an ETS bus pull out from the curb in front of the building where The Express live when I hear the crash of glass break and look up to see

Melvin Rattlesnake flash through the mauve light of the streetlight. White as winter, he just for a second light up the sky like lightning.

manitou motors

Merton Wolfchild always been kind of a hero of mine. The year I was ten or eleven they held the Alberta Golden Gloves Boxing Championships in the Camrose High School Auditorium. In them days, boxers from our reserve, The Hobbema Boxing Club, was known all over the province as really good fighters, and Merton Wolfchild was the best of them.

He weren't very tall but he was built solid and move quick as a cat. Merton's skin was the colour of new cowboy boots and just as shiny. His eyes be set real wide apart and he say that make him able to see real good from sideways. He alway got one piece of black hair that keep falling down over his face like a shoelace. Boy, the final bout of the 150 lb. fighters was the best I ever seen. The RCMP guys from Wetaskiwin have their own boxing club and Merton he fought a Constable Pike. That Constable Pike don't look near so scary wearing nothing but blue boxing shorts and gloves, as he do all decked up in his uniform and carry a gun.

Merton close up one of Constable Pike's eyes in the first round and about halfway through the second he knock him right on the seat of his pants. Boy, I stand up and cheer for Merton loud as my voice will go, until a lady in a red mackinaw who sit in front of me turn around and say, "Try not to yell so loud in my ear, Kid." In the third round, Merton he knock out that Constable Pike. Hit him with a right on the chin and boy his head hit the floor of the ring like a sack of feed thrown into an empty wagon box. His RCMP friends have to carry the Constable back to his corner.

There be a big celebration down to the bar of the Coronation Hotel in Camrose that night and Merton sure be a hero around the reserve for a while. He got presented with a big trophy with a gold boxer about six inches high on it, and it used to sit around the table at Wolfchild's cabin until it got all dusty: then the little kids played with it, and finally it just disappeared.

Merton never boxed no more that I know of except to fight in the Alice Hotel bar once in a while or out in the yard at Blue Quills Dance Hall at Hobbema after everybody got drunked up some, even though everybody say he could of been one of those professional boxers if he'd of wanted to. Couple of years later he moved over to Camrose to live, that be thirty or so miles from the reserve. I heard he married with a white girl and be selling cars up there.

I wish I'd never heard that. Cause when my friend Norman Scar work all winter in the lumber camp and save his money to buy a car, it is me who suggests that we should go to Camrose and find Merton Wolfchild. I figure that if anybody not going to cheat us it be another Indian. Indians have a bad time buying cars. White salesmen always seem to cheat them one way or another.

Once I walk around Honest Ernie's Used Car Lot in Wetaskiwin and I hear a couple of salesmen say about a '57 Dodge with big fenders that painted pink and black and got white seats and a monkey on a stick in the back window: "That's a wahoo special." And sure enough a couple of weeks later I seen the car around the reserve, but not for long. Pretty quick the transmission and most everything else go on it and it been sit for a long time in a slough down a ways from our cabins.

Bunch of us pile in Louis Coyote's pickup truck and drive up to Camrose. There's me and Norman Scar, my friend Frank Fence-post, my girlfriend Sadie One-wound, Frank's girlfriend Connie Bigcharles, Norman's sister Julie, and two or three other guys who ride in the back of the truck after the cab be all full.

Camrose ain't all that much bigger than Wetaskiwin so it's not that hard to drive around the used car lots until we find one that got an Indian salesman. The sign say, Manitou Motors, easy credit, no down payments, and it got a picture of a tall Indian girl wear only a tiny bathing suit and a red-and-white war bonnet. It sure look like a big business to us as we pull the truck up to the curb. There be rows and rows of light bulbs in red, yellow and blue, and between the rows of bulbs is lines of plastic triangles in bright colours that blow in the wind and make noise like a whole lot of guys snapping their fingers. There must be 30 cars on the lot all shiny and fresh washed.

Merton spot us right away and he come down to meet us, shake our hands and say hello to us in Cree. Norman Scar be pretty shy with strangers so I have to tell Merton that it is my friend who wants to buy a car.

Merton Wolfchild sure ain't the way I remember him from back when he used to box. He put on lots of weight and some of it hang over his belt quite a ways. He got on a white shirt, black pants and some pretty old cowboy boots. He have a wide brown belt with a big square buckle have a picture of a bottle of Lethbridge Pale Ale on it.

"You guys just make yourself at home," he say, and wave his hand around the lot. "When you find something you like, let me know and I let you take it out for a ride." It easy to see that Merton's nose been busted a couple of times and he got a pretty bad scar on one cheek. I don't remember none of that from when I knew him before.

Frank Fence-post, him and Connie Bigcharles be climb in and out of cars like they look for something. It look like they maybe gonna try for set a record for sit in every car on the lot in maybe ten minutes.

"I used to watch you box," I tell Merton.

"Yeah?" he say, and give me a big smile. "Those were the days."

"I seen you the time you knocked out Constable Pike. I cheered so loud for you I didn't have no voice for a couple of days."

"You know something, Norman," he says to me, "That Constable Pike guy is still trying to get even on me. He be stationed up here now and he come around the lot give me tickets for no safety stickers on my cars, and he always digging up some new regulations that he say I broke some time or other."

"I'm Silas Ermineskin," I tell him just to straighten things out. But at least he remembered the name of the guy who want to buy the car.

"You must be Paul's kid maybe. You got a real pretty sister . . . Elaine? or . . ."

"Illianna," I say. "She's married with a white man and lives in Calgary."

"Too bad, I kind of had my eye on her one time. Well, I married with a white girl. We got four kids."

"This is sure a fancy car lot you got here."

"Yeah, well I think it's kind of nice. It make me a good living."

Merton talk like he own it but I see by the licence on the wall of his office that it be some other name listed as own Manitou Motors Ltd.

"So Constable Pike still trying to get even for get beat up by you?"

"Yes, sir, I'm gonna have to punch him out again one of these days," and Merton smack one fist into his other hand and laugh real loud.

Most everybody but Norman and Julie has followed us up to the office. Merton take a cigarette package out of his shirt pocket and pass them around to everybody.

"After your friend decide on a car we all have us a drink to celebrate," he say, "How much money has your friend got to spend?"

"$800," I tell him.

"Well for that I can get him one really good car, Norman," he say and slap my shoulder. "Us Hobbema Indians got to stick together. I sure glad you came to me instead of to some white bugger that rip you off."

Up at the front of the lot Merton is got built a little platform that have a nice sports car sit up on it, have a sign on the windshield say, Special of the Day, just like the Gold Nugget Café in Wetaskiwin have a grilled cheese sandwich and cole slaw for 99 cents. Frank and Connie and Norman all be up on that platform and have the hood up on the car. Now if there is one thing Frank be really good at it is start up a car without have no keys. We hear the motor go backfire a couple of times and then start up. Connie Bigcharles who sit behind the steering wheel get all excited and put the car into gear and it be drive off across the country except that the back wheels catch on the edge of the platform and the car just sit there like it going down a really steep hill. They be awful lucky that they don't kill Frank or even Eddy Crier who was stand in front of the platform and have to jump like hell to get out of the way in time.

I figure that that sure ain't a very smart thing to do especially when a Golden Glove Champion owns that car. I figure that Merton probably gonna pound those guys good. But he just have a big laugh about it, once he see that the car ain't hurt none. He gets all us guys down front and we lift that little car back up where it should be.

"Hey, partner," Merton say to Frank, "you let me start up the cars around here, okay?"

Norman come up to me real quiet and he look at the ground. "I seen one that I like, Silas," and he point over to where his sister Julie is stand beside a yellow-and-black

Ford 4-door, got no hub caps and a pretty bad scratch along one fender. "You asks him for me how much it is?"

"My friend like the yellow Ford over there," I tell Merton. "How much you charge him for it?"

Merton make a sad face. "That one be a thousand bucks," he says, but then he stop and scratch his head and that shoelace of hair fall down over his face. "Seeing as you guys are brothers and all, and seeing as how you cheered for me when I whipped Constable Pike, I sell it to youse guys for $795, and I throw in the licence plates."

Norman shake happy and kick some gravel around.

"First though, we want to drive it around," I say.

"I can see you got a good business head, Norman," Merton say to me. "You guys come on inside the office and we fix up the papers so's you can test drive it."

I introduce everybody around again and make sure that he know that Norman is Norman and I'm Silas. The office is pretty tiny. Just a couple of desks, four or five chairs and heater. It be built out of cedar and smell good to the nose.

Merton he takes a long time fill out forms and stuff, and he have to cross out a lot and he have a hard time spell an easy name like Norman Scar. Finally he get Norman to sign in about five places and he have Norman leave with him his $800, just to be sure we don't run off to Montana with the car, he say with a big laugh. When all that is done Merton say we be able to test drive the car, but first Merton pull out a whisky bottle from the desk drawer, take a big drink, then he pass the bottle around to each of us. We thank him for the drink.

"What are friends for?" he say, and pass cigarettes around again.

Frank, he already got the car started when we get out there with the keys. But Merton he still in a good mood and say, "Take it for a spin around town but be careful that Constable Pike don't give you no tickets." He's had a couple more drinks from the bottle and starting to feel pretty good.

Norman Scar and me is the only ones who got drivers' licences, so Norman drive us off down the street after all nine of us get settled in the car. "Why don't we head up to Edmonton," Frank say, "the sales guy don't say when we have to be back. We make a party up there and come back tomorrow or the next day?" Norman probably go along with that but I tell them we just test the car. We can go anyplace we want after it been bought.

The car seem to me to run pretty rough. After a while I get Norman to let me drive it. It got a standard transmission and the clutch don't catch until it all the way out, and I think a couple of cogs be broken off second gear. The steering be pretty loose too. But Norman says he likes the colour of the car and the soft red seat covers and say he thinks he buy it.

I run it up to about 50 mph and it just about shimmy me right off the road but Norman ain't about to change his mind.

I notice that it's running pretty hot, so as we pull up in front of the car lot I give the clutch a pretty good kick and stall the motor. Then just like I figure, when I turn the key it don't start. I argue a little with Norman and tell him to try some other cars first before he buy this one and he finally agree with me.

Merton come down to meet us flipping his hair out of his eyes and smiling.

"I don't think we buy this one, Mr. Wolfchild," I tell him. "Maybe we'd like to look at the white Chevy over there."

"That one's way too expensive for you," Merton say, and he scratch his head real hard. "I tell you what I do. I throw in a radio, and a tape deck, and hell, what are friends for, I'll even give you a couple of tapes. Take them right out of my own collection. I mean after all you guys are from my home town."

Norman just about to say okay, but I butt in. "This ain't a very good car, Mr. Wolfchild. I been working on engines down to the Technical School at Wetaskiwin for most of two years now, and I can tell there's lots of things wrong with this car."

"Five tapes, and that's my final offer. Two Merle Haggard, a Waylon Jennings, one each of Dolly Parton and Donna Fargo."

"The car don't even start no more and I think the clutch has gone out."

"It was okay when you took it out. Besides there ain't nothing else on the lot that you guys can afford. And why don't you let the buyer talk for himself," and he kind of elbow me out of the way. "Tell you what I do, and this is final," he say to Norman, "I give you one of them big chrome feet to put where your gas pedal is. Costs $12 wholesale at Midland Auto Supply. How about it Silas?"

He'd of had himself a deal if he hadn't mixed up the names again, cause Norman had his mouth all shaped to say yes.

"No, sir. I don't think so. I think we look around some more," Norman say in a small whisper.

Well, Merton step back and kind of take up a pose like he used to when he was a boxer. "Look, kid, I thought you understood. You bought the car. We made a deal in there a while ago. You got yourself a car. Now I'll still throw in the extras I promised, but you own the car, okay? Once you sign a deal there's no backing out of it."

"But he just signed it to test drive it," I say.

"Who asked you?" Merton say to me in a real nasty voice, and I see he got his fists clenched.

Boy I sure don't know what to do. We all just stand around for a while until Merton flip that hair out of his eyes and say he going to round up the tapes and chrome gas pedal and all. He put the radio and tape deck in the trunk, say we can get it hooked up by somebody who know how.

We all try for a while to start that Ford up but even Frank can't get it going. "It be okay in an hour or so," Merton say. "It just run a little hot is all."

We sit around in Louis Coyote's pickup, smoke cigarettes and try to figure what to do. I tell Norman I sure is sorry for suggest we come here.

Then I start thinking about Constable Pike and I tell

everybody about the idea I have, but they sure don't think much of it, cause us Indians the less we have to do with the RCMP guys the happier it makes both us and them.

There be a thunderstorm blowing up and all of a sudden it got as dark and windy as the inside of a nose. Them flags snap loud and there be lots of dirt blow around the streets.

Nobody wants to use my idea so I let them all go and sit in Norman's car and I take my girlfriend Sadie One-wound and the truck and drive over to the RCMP headquarters.

Constable Pike seem a lot bigger than I remember him. He got a red face like a polished apple and his boots slap loud on the floor when he walk.

"I'll come down and investigate," he say to me after I explain what has happened, "but I can't promise anything. Your friend Norman could take the company to court and probably get his money back but he'd have to go to a lot of trouble to do it. That's what men like Burge and Wolfchild count on."

"Who's this guy Burge?"

"He owns Manitou Motors. Merton Wolfchild married his daughter. Guess Burge figures it's better to have him working there than to support his daughter and all those kids of Merton's."

While we been in the RCMP office it rained real hard with thunder and lightning, but by the time we got over there, us in the truck and Constable Pike in his black-and-white car, only a few drops be fall and the sun start to come out again.

The windows of the Ford be fogged up tight and the only way we can tell there is people in there is by the cigarette smoke come out of the vent window.

"How much did you say he charged you for that car?" the Constable ask.

"$800," I tell him.

"It's worth about $250 at the very most. No wonder he was trying to buy you off with a tape deck and other junk."

Merton come march down from his office and meet us about the middle of the car lot. "So what you gonna pick on me about today?" he say to Constable Pike.

"Boys here claim they only wanted to test drive the car."

"They're just sore cause it don't run as good as they thought. I sell my cars as-is-here-is. No refunds. No weaseling out of a deal."

"I suppose the car's got a safety sticker. You know it's illegal to sell a car without one."

"I got the papers someplace."

"I suggest you go find them. And I think we should test the tires. It's illegal to sell a car with less than $\frac{1}{8}$ inch of tread on the tires."

"You gonna put me in jail for selling bald tires? That be about your speed. You make it damn hard for a poor Indian to make a living."

Merton get uglier as he go along but Constable Pike keep pretty cool. While I been away this Mr. Burge fellow is turn up. He look about 60 and wear a baggy grey suit, and have a lean face that come to a sharp point like a fox.

"Maybe you should give back the money," he say a couple of times. "We don't want no more trouble with cops." But he just hang around on the edge of things like an animal waiting for something to die.

They argue for a while more. It don't look like we gonna get that money back. Then Constable Pike get out his book and say he gonna write out tickets for no safety stickers and thin tires and he start to look around the lot at the other cars, saying he might as well check all of them while he here.

Merton jump about a foot off the ground. "You put me out of business," he yell. "No stinking cop gonna do that to me."

Merton he make a fist and raise up his hand to hit Constable Pike but before any of us know for sure what happened Merton be sitting on the seat of his pants in the wet gravel, feel with one hand at his chin, and look around like somebody asked him a real hard question.

Things move pretty quick after that. Mr. Burge he get the money from Merton's back pocket and give it to Norman, and then he get the papers from inside the office and tear them up for everybody to see. He say a lot of nice things to Constable Pike, and say that him and Merton promise to be good from now on if the Constable don't charge Merton with trying to hit him. I notice though that he never once look in Constable Pike's face while he saying all this.

We all head for the pickup truck, figure the sooner we get out of town the better. Louis Coyote's pickup ain't got no safety sticker and all four tires be so thin that a good healthy mosquito bite them into a blow-out.

Constable Pike is taking down numbers off all the cars on the lot.

Mr. Burge is yell loud at Merton for getting caught at do something bad.

"But they were Indians," Merton is say, spread his arms real wide. "I don't figure for them to make no trouble. You just can't trust anybody no more."

the forest

"When I was six or seven, bunch of us guys take a blanket from Blind Louis' cabin and we take turns swing each other around with a guy on each corner and one in the middle. When my turn for the middle come, the guys think it be funny to wrap me up, tie the corners together and leave me. The blanket was thick grey wool. It was dark and hot and I hear the noises from outside but can't tell the direction they come from. I tear at that blanket with my hands, try to get me some air and some eyesight, but can't. I cry some. The sweat run off me and I figure I gonna die for sure until I remember my jack knife. It be one I found and got only one broke blade, but I be able to poke it through the wool and cut myself out. I never forgot what the air feel like on my face, and that the first thing I can smell is the forest, the spruce trees."

Allen Threepersons is the guy who say all that. We is sit in the bar of the Hub Hotel on a Saturday afternoon and have us a few beers, and he tell me that story cause I ask how he liked to live all the time in the city. We both been raised up on the reserve at Hobbema. Allen be about 25 now. He went off to work in the lumber camps when he was about 16. Used to be he'd winter there and live his summers on the reserve. Then a couple of year ago he married up with a white girl named Janey, and they come to live here in Edmonton all the year cause that where Janey want to live.

"I hate the goddamned city, Silas. I need me the smell of the forest. I can't breathe here. Look at this here bar, it ain't got no windows. After a while the city just kind of wrap itself around you."

Him and Janey got themselves two rooms in an apartment right on Jasper Avenue, main street of Edmonton, upstairs from the Dreamland Dance Hall. Wednesday and Saturday nights you be able to feel the music come lift up through the building, about the same as the smell of cabbage do every day. Those nights the building creak some when the band play fast music and everyone jump up and down.

The rooms Allen and Janey got is like live in a vacant place. Two big square rooms make their furniture look like it off in the distance someplace. They got an old black gas stove, a table, only two chairs so when three of us in the kitchen one have to stand up. The other room have a mattress on the floor with a radio beside it and a saucer for an ashtray. There be a real old sofa chair with a torn green cover, and a crib for their baby, Tommy. It be one made by hand by a bad carpenter. It got crooked slats and a big pillow for a mattress. That room smell like the baby.

On the wall Allen hung his big double-bit axe: birch handle smooth and the colour of fine blond hair. The blade be blue as moonlight and shine like the holy pictures I seen at St. Andrew's Catholic Church one time.

Janey don't have no idea how to make that a cheerful place. There be no curtains on the window that look back on another part of the building, and down on an alley where delivery trucks plough through the heavy snow, make it rutted and brown as a ploughed field.

Since they live in the city, Allen he mostly not working. Indians have a hard time get jobs anytime, but not much work for loggers in town.

After we drink our beer we go up to Allen's rooms that be only a block from the bar. I be up here in Edmonton take some course that the Government offer on how to be a mechanic. Go to school usually at Wetaskiwin about ten mile from the reserve, but this here course I got to take not offered down there.

Allen Threepersons be both bigger and taller than me, and I'm most six foot tall and don't have to be afraid of too many people. His arms be as big as the tops of my legs and when he buy clothes they have to be the extra-large size. He have kind of a fierce face with a big nose, not round, but long and sharp like the roof of a dog house. His teeth be shiny and white, so hard he can open the caps of beer bottles with them.

His being strong and handsome is, I suppose, why Janey like him. Don't know so much about her. Allen meet her in Edson or Hinton; towns close to the lumber camp where he used to work. She look to me like maybe one of them white girls who get stuck on Indian guys, any Indian guy. She got fair skin and yellow hair, but that awful yellow like the colour they paint fire engines, and it show black down close to her head. Her teeth be small, close together, and look like they been filed down on something. I don't like to see her smile.

The next Monday, after my class, I go with Allen over to the Kelly Man Temporary Employment Office. Once in a while he get in a day unload cement bags or some other kind of railroad car. Today there ain't nothing doing at the employment office, but on the way back we meet up with Eli Gauthier, a logger that I know a little bit but Allen knows a lot.

"They're hiring over to the IWA Hall," he says to Allen.

"Yeah! For where?"

"Up Fort McMurray way. Steady work until spring. Good wages too."

"Naw. My old lady say she can't stand to be left alone."

"Hey, this here's a Government logging camp," say Eli. "Whole little town there. They got houses for married guys and they take your word for it. No marriage licence or nothing. I taking Brenda Littlechild with me."

Well, Allen give a couple of little jumps, throw back his head and breathe up at what sky he can see between the trolley wires.

"Let's go over to Union Hall," he say. "By God, me and Janey both be able to get what we want."

Allen sign up for work in the logging camp, which be what he want. Janey, I have to wait and see. She ain't home when we get back. The baby be asleep with a bottle. On the table is a tin of canned milk and an empty beer bottle. The milk can got two tracks like yellow shoe laces run down all the way to the table top.

Janey finally come back from have a beer with some friends. "If I knew for sure you guys was back I could have stayed," she say. "I suppose you're mad at me for leaving the baby alone," she say to Allen.

"Not this time," he say, and quick tell her all about his new job, and how he don't have to leave her and Tommy, but can take them along.

"One bar and a two-hole outhouse," say Janey, and make a pouty face as she light up a cigarette. "I told you when we got married that I wanted to live in the city. I hate little towns and camps . . ." and, boy, she go on about that for about ten minutes.

While she talking, Janey put right on over her jeans and sweater a pink-coloured dressing-gown be so bright you have to blink your eyes. The baby's made messes down the front of it and it smell bad clear across the room to where I am. Wednesday and Saturday, Janey have her hair up in pink rollers all day. At night, she put on a dress look like it made out of green leaves of some kind, silver high heels, take her cigarettes and go downstairs to dance. Allen hardly ever go with her cause he don't like for leave Tommy alone. Janey almost pretty, dress up like that, except that tight dress push her belly out too much.

I don't know what the hell Allen see in her. I'd like to ask, but it ain't none of my business. I know love sometime make you see people not the way they really is, and for a while you do things you don't want to, just so it please them.

Allen try to talk soft on her but she keep on be sulky. I feel bad for him cause he want so much to share some of his happy with her. He go and take his axe off the wall, swing it back and forth some, be careful not to hit nothing.

"The forest," he say to me, and smile big.

For all the noise she make, Janey don't say that she not going to go.

"Tomorrow we go get some warm clothes for you and Tommy," Allen say, wetting his finger and testing the edge of his axe blade.

"You should go out cut down a few parking meters just to practise up for the big trees," I say, and Allen and me have a good laugh.

"I got to take Tommy to the clinic tomorrow," say Janey. "I forgot the last two times I was supposed to go."

Next day I meet Allen after class and we shop around for a while, price hard hats and steel-toed boots. Allen he cash his unemployment cheque and he buy for Janey a yellow woolly sweater be about the same colour as her hair. On the way back to his place we stop for a beer and Allen be so happy that he buy up a round for a couple of guys he don't even know.

Janey's already back from the clinic and she got her chin up in the air and hardly even look at the present Allen brought her.

"I'm pregnant again," she say, blowing smoke across the table at Allen. "Doctor says I shouldn't go out to the bush. Gotta stay close to the clinic," and she smile with them little short teeth of hers.

Allen take that a lot better than I figured. He hang his

axe back up on the wall and then I walk with him over to the Union Hall where he get unsigned for the job.

We walk slow back to his place. His shoulders be bent over some and he walk like he carry something on his back. Outside the bar of the Hub Hotel, there be on the street by the door two Indian kids, boy about four hold on to the hand of a girl about two. Her little legs bow some the way babies' do. She got on just a light skirt and wool sweater. The boy has jeans and the same kind of sweater. They wait where they been told to, just walk back and forth on the packed snow.

"Look at them," Allen say. He stoop over and say something to them in Cree, but they don't understand.

"Look at them," he say again. "It could . . ." but he don't finish the sentence. He just kick his boots hard at the snow on the sidewalk.

Next morning, I on my way catch the bus to the Tech School. It some below zero, cold fog hang in the air and the snow crunch loud under my boots on the sidewalk. As I come up to the Dreamland Dance Hall I see police cars, and people stand around in a circle, blow out their breath like white flowers. Them people raise up on their toes to make their necks longer. The police is talk in low voices to some of the people. One is a guy with a gold tooth and a nose like a pump handle, that I know own the building.

"Crazy goddam Indian," I hear him say. "Look at my door. Just look at my door."

And sure enough the door be all chopped to pieces. Big enough hole for people step right in and out but the door knob be still there and so is the hinges.

"Bugger went running right across Jasper Avenue there, damn near got hit by a bus," somebody else say. "Way he was running and waving that axe he'd have chopped up the bus too if it got in his way."

"Last I seen of him he went legging it down into the river valley," say a man with thick glasses. And everybody look across the street and down to where the Saskatchewan River lay froze like a big white snake.

"Wasn't even wearing a shirt," I hear someone say as I push my way into the building where the dirty stairs run straight up for about 50 feet. The door to Allen's room be chopped up same as the one downstairs and I can hear the baby, Tommy Threepersons, crying. Janey is hold the baby to her by one arm around his middle. She wear that bright pink dressing-gown with fuzz long as porcupine quills. Her yellow-coloured hair ain't been combed and it hang around her head in ropes thick as battery cables.

"What happened?" I ask.

She shrug her shoulder some and nod her head to the door. It easy to see by her eyes that she don't understand none of what's happened to her.

"He was drinking his coffee . . . he just took that axe . . . 'The forest, the forest,' was all he said . . . everytime he brought the axe down he said it."

black wampum

"Billy Jawbone's gonna give away his baby girl!" Frank Fence-post say as he come puffing down the hill to where a bunch of us raking and coiling hay. I got my shirt off and the sweat run into my eyes and down my back. The air be so thick with red clover that the taste of it get right into my mouth. Nobody say anything right away so Frank keep on, "I heard him say so myself just a few minutes ago down at the store at Hobbema."

"Black wampum," say Mad Etta.

Etta is taking a rest. She sitting down with her big legs straight out in front of her. Mad Etta be our medicine man on the Ermineskin Reserve, and she work right along with us at haying.

"Black wampum, that's what Billy said," say Frank. "What's it mean?"

"Silas can tell you," say Etta, and look over at me.

I supposed to be Etta's assistant medicine man. She promise to learn me all the secrets of be a doctor. I read about black wampum one time in a whiteman book, only they called it forced adoption.

I try to explain but I got clover seeds stick to the back of my neck and inside the waist of my jeans and I do more scratch than talking until Mad Etta take over.

"When Indian tribes used to be at war with each other, sometime they catch prisoners. Instead of kill them they give them to families that lost sons in the war. New family treats the prisoner like he was a relative and the prisoner usually try to make himself fit in cause he'd rather be that than dead." Etta smile her big smile show where some teeth used to be in her face.

"That be a pretty good idea," say Frank. "Wonder why white men don't use that instead of having jails."

"I suppose he gonna give it to the Winemullers," I say.

"He didn't say," says Frank, "but he say to tell Mad Etta that he want to see her tonight. He wants her to make arrangement for him."

Frank say this to me but Mad Etta sit right there and listen. Mad Etta look up at me and grin as she wipe the sweat off her forehead.

"Silas, I just have a vision," she say. "I dream that Frank Fence-post gonna come here and tell me Billy Jawbone want to see me tonight," and she laugh and laugh.

Frank take himself a drink from the water bucket and pour a little over his head. He always been a little scared of Mad Etta since one time she throwed him right through the screen door of her cabin cause he was making fun on something she was doing.

"I suppose it make Billy feel better in himself to do that, but what about Mrs. Jawbone?" I say to Mad Etta.

"You getting smart, Silas. My guess is she be the one we have to worry about."

"While we are talking Frank is chase away a few dogs that come sneak around the place where we got our sandwiches stashed. The land we are haying on used to belong to a family called Crowchild who moved off the reserve a couple of years ago and left a half dozen or so dogs around the place.

"Never figured Billy Jawbone to be one to go back to the old ways," I say.

"Peoples do funny things to survive," say Etta. "Not only peoples," she say, and point over to where Frank is wave a stick at the dogs. A couple of them is down on their bellies, ears flat and growling so I can see the pink of their lips rolled back from their teeth. Another couple of dogs are sort of slinking in the tall grass making circles and coming in from the side.

"Them dogs been forced to go back to their wild ways to stay alive," say Etta. Indians sometime a lot like animals, we ain't been away from our wild ways for very long.

Until about three weeks ago Billy Jawbone was working on a farm up north of Wetaskiwin for a German family called Winemuller. Just doing chores, chopping wood and stuff like that, when one day he back the John Deere tractor from the machine shed and run over the Winemuller's baby. They say that the tractor wheel crushed him flat just like it been a doll he runned over. The kid was named Wayne and only been a year or so old. He walked away when his mother turned her back for a minute.

I seen the Winemuller couple around town sometimes. They be heavy, onion-faced people, stocky as stooks. They're probably about 30 and this is their only baby.

When people on the reserve hear about the accident happen they borrow Louis Coyote's pickup truck and drive Jean Jawbone up to the RCMP office in Wetaskiwin to be with Billy.

RCMP hang around the farm there all day, take pictures, make plaster prints of the tires, get Billy to tell his story a couple of dozen times. Finally the RCMP decide that it ain't Billy's fault. At all. Not even gonna have an inquest, they say. If the RCMP don't blame the Indian in an accident you got to figure that he was at least 100% right, or more.

I'm at Mad Etta's cabin that night when Billy come to see her. Billy lived all his life on the reserve. Like most of us guys he work at cut brush from the railroad right-of-ways, in a lumber camp, or for farmers, maybe.

"You sure you want to do this?" Mad Etta say.

"Don't want to. I got to."

Billy is kind of tobacco-coloured, thin, with deep-set eyes. He wear tight jeans, boots, a blue work shirt and a black cowboy hat tied under his chin with a yellow string.

"What's Jean think?"

"I ain't told her."

"You want me to?"

"Yeah. First you see if Mr. Winemuller will take the baby. Don't want Jean to know unless it really going to happen."

But I think Jean Jawbone got a pretty good idea already. She spent most every night for the last couple of weeks in the beer parlour of the Alice Hotel in Wetaskiwin. I give her a ride home one night when I seen her walking drunk down the highway. Jean ain't much to look at. She be short, got a flat face and she never put no curl in her hair or wear lipstick or nothing. She got a puffy belly and she walk the funny way that pregnant ladies do, except she not pregnant.

She only mumble some the night I drove her home, but I never know her to be one to drink a whole lot, and she sure ain't happy drunk the way people supposed to get after a lot of beer.

"Police say you didn't do nothing wrong. How come you feel you got to give them your baby?" Mad Etta say to Billy.

"You weren't there to see what the baby look like after I run over him." Billy take a long drink of his beer. His adam's apple run up and down his skinny neck when he swallow. "Pushed right down flat into the ground and there was blood bust out of him in almost every place on his body."

"You didn't mean to hurt him."

"In the old days if an Indian kill somebody, even by accident, the one who done the killing had to take the dead

Indian's place with his family. I'd go myself but what would Mr. Winemuller want with a growed-up Indian? But I can give Tammy to them."

Mad Etta shrug her big buffalo shoulder. "If you got your mind closed up on the idea, then Silas and me, we see what we can do. What church do they go to? We go and look up their medicine man."

I remember one time down at the Tech School in Wetaskiwin, Mr. Nichols got to talking about this here Greek guy who walked around carrying a lantern and looking for an honest man.

"Honesty is relative," I hear Mr. Nichols say.

"Like a cousin or uncle?" Frank Fence-post whisper loud into my ear.

I punch Frank's arm and tell him to shut up, but by then I lost what it is that Mr. Nichols trying to say. I think maybe it is something about honesty is different things to different peoples.

Seem to me that a person can't get much more honest than Billy Jawbone, but when I tell Mad Etta about it and suggest that they should of sent that guy with the lantern out here to the Ermineskin Reserve, she wrinkle up her nose and look at me like I five years old and naked.

First thing next day I get Frank and Rufus to help load Mad Etta into the back of Blind Louis Coyote's pickup truck and we drive up to the Christ on the Cross Lutheran Church in Wetaskiwin. Etta and me go in.

It be a new church just built a couple of years ago, smell inside like varnish and running shoes. The Rev. Beyer have a desk like I seen down to the Toronto-Dominion Bank, half purple and half yellow, and the walls of his office be the same colour and got hanging on them pictures drawed by little kids. When we tell him why we there the Rev. Beyer scratch his head and say about six or seven times that he never heard of such a thing. He get on the phone to the RCMP ask if it legal for Billy to do that. All them RCMP guys will say is that it don't appear to be illegal. I bet they running around *their* offices scratching *their* heads and saying they never heard of such a thing.

The Rev. Beyer is kind of a soft-looking man, his shoulders be stooped some, I guess from stand and hold the bible in his hands for so much of the time.

We take the reverend in the pickup truck out to Winemuller's farm. I bet they sure surprised to see their minister get out of a whole truckful of Indians. The Winemullers stand beside each other in front of the house as Rev. Beyer explain that Billy Jawbone want to give them his little girl, Tammy, to take the place of the baby that he runned over. I can smell bread baking from inside the house.

Rev. Beyer try to get Winemullers to say no to the idea. He explain that what Billy doing ain't recognized by law so that any time he could come and take Tammy back and they could do nothing legal about it.

Winemuller say at first that he don't think it is a good idea, but his wife got a hold of his arm with both hands and I bet he have fingerprints for a week she holding him so hard. Mrs. Winemuller wear glasses so thick that I can't see but a blue blur for her eyes.

"How old is she?" Mrs. Winemuller ask in a real choked voice. She got flour on her hands and arms and a streak of white on one cheek where she wiped a hand.

"Eight months," say Etta.

"Maybe God meant for us to have her," she say to her husband, and she look at Rev. Beyer like she dare him to say it ain't so. "I can't have no more babies myself," she say and wipe her face on her husband's sleeve.

Winemuller agree that they going to pray on it and let Rev. Beyer know that evening, but I can tell by the way they look that they going to say yes.

"You saying I'd break my word?" Billy say to Rev. Beyer after the reverend give him that speech about it being legal or not. We are sitting, Etta, Billy, the reverend and me, in the Gold Nugget Café in Wetaskiwin.

"No. I'm sure your intentions are good but you are very overwrought emotionally. You might reconsider, or your wife could also take legal action without your permission."

"Tonight I have my wife sewing up the black wampum," say Billy. "What I do be just as permanent as the Wine-muller kid be dead."

"How come you don't tell Winemullers that it maybe kill Jean Jawbone if they take her baby away?" I say to Mad Etta that night.

"You saw that they was gonna say yes, right? What good would it do to make them feel guilty too. A snake and a buzz-saw wouldn't of stopped that woman from taking a baby offered to her."

"Nooooo . . ." Jean Jawbone cry when Mad Etta finally get around to telling her what's going to happen. The wailing sound Jean make I bet can be heard for half a mile.

"Why couldn't you tell me yourself?" she screech at Billy, but she don't wait for him to answer. "I know something bad gonna happen." Then she turn to Etta and me. "He ain't touched Tammy since the accident, and he keep tell about how his grandfather told him about this here black wampum stuff."

The yelling waked up Tammy, the baby, and Jean pick her up from her bed. The baby yawn and rub her nose on her mama's shoulder.

"Damn you and your old ways," Jean yell at Billy and Etta and me. And she tell us to get out of her cabin before she get the shotgun after us. But Jean don't make no move to get the shotgun so we don't make no motions of leaving. Etta start in to talk a lot to try and calm Jean down some.

"Old ways aren't always better. I like to go to the Safeway Store in Wetaskiwin buy up five pounds of hamburger instead of have to go out and kill a buffalo for dinner," say Etta and she stop and laugh. "Another thing I'm glad is gone is the cutting. Old-time Indian women used to cut their arms and legs with sharp flint or a knife when they mourning for a dead relative. Some of them even used to cut off one joint from a finger every time a relative died. Government outlawed that back even before I was born. If that be in style now, Etta have nothing but a thumb left on each hand. How the hell would I ever roll me a cigarette?" And she laugh and laugh and her body seem to move around inside her dress like a half-full sack of grain.

Etta go on for a long time and I listen close but I sure don't understand how she do what she do. She let both Billy and Jean know that she understand how they feel but she don't tell either one of them what they should or shouldn't do.

Word around the reserve kind of travel on the wind and before long most everyone know that Billy going to give away his baby come Saturday. Most Indian people leave folks alone to solve their problems. They figure that they got enough trouble of their own without butt into other people's. Then there is Bedelia Coyote. She play Helen Reddy records on her phonograph, get mail from Feminist News Service and wear blue-tinted glasses. She come down to see Jean Jawbone on Thursday night. Jean be sitting at the kitchen table sewing on the black wampum.

Black wampum just be black beads sewed on a piece of buckskin that be fitted to the shoulders of the person who going to be adopted. It look about the same as the thing that priests wear over their shoulders. Guess the priests copied from the Indians cause at least around here there been Indians a lot longer than a Catholic church.

"Tomorrow we gonna take you up to Edmonton see a white lawyer," say Bedelia. "He put a stop quick to this dumb idea." Then she light into Billy, tell him when he start having babies all by himself then he be able to decide what to do with them.

"We're only Indians," say Jean. "Lawyers don't do nothing for Indians."

"The hell they don't," say Bedelia. "You're giving away an Indian, and to white people at that. If you let him do it your baby's gonna grow up white."

Bedelia is so mad she is yelling loud.

"I fix things my own way," say Jean, and keep on sewing the black wampum, and she say it in a voice like she don't care one way or another.

Bedelia keep yelling for most an hour but it don't do no

good.

We stop the truck at the gate to Winemuller's farm. The sun is hot and shines sharp off the windshield of the pickup truck making my eyes squint when I look back down the lane. There be barbed-wire fence along both sides of the road for about a hundred yards and then Winemuller's house sit on the left. The wheat is blond and ready for harvest.

As we walk up the dusty road we go in kind of an uneven line. Billy Jawbone wearing his beaded buckskin shirt and with his hat down over his eyes, carries Tammy. She wearing a white flannel dress and over her shoulder, like a bib fastened on both front and back, is the black wampum that her mother made. Tammy smile and coo and reach out her fat hands the way babies do, like she try to catch butterflies that ain't there.

I hang back off to the left some. Then there is Jean Jawbone who walk like maybe she been given some strong drug. She wearing jeans, running shoes and a bright pink sweater that shrink some and show an inch or two of her belly above her jeans. She slump along kind of dazed but her eyes are wild and she ain't combed her hair today. Mad Etta puff along behind Jean. Etta's breath sound like a cow that just run across a field for a mile or so. Way behind are Frank and Rufus. We only need them to help load and unload Etta from the truck. They can't decide whether to stay or come along. Frank got in the pocket of his jean jacket a transistor radio and we must be half-way up the lane before I can't hear it anymore. There is a little bit of hot breeze blow in our faces and I can smell the leather of Billy's jacket mixed with the wheat smell.

Up in front of the house, which be greyish-coloured and got a broken TV antenna hang from the roof like the skeleton of a bird, stand the Winemullers and the Rev. Beyer from the Christ on the Cross Lutheran Church. Winemuller got his big arms folded across his bib overalls and from this far away he look bald because his hair be so light coloured. Mrs. Winemuller, stocky as her husband, wear a dress the same colour as the fat Plymouth-rocks hens that dust themselves in the dirt.

From the angle I look at Billy Jawbone it don't appear like he got any front to his face. It just look like the sides of his face come to an edge like an axe blade. His skin be stretched tight and golden over his cheekbones. The Rev. Beyer, black as a charred tree, stand with his neck bent forward and the Bible held tight in his hands.

Billy is still about twenty yards from the Winemullers when Jean let out a bird-sound kind of cry like maybe something inside her broke. She run up to Billy's side and take from the sheath on his belt his hunting knife. I sure afraid for what she might do. Billy keep on walking like he don't even notice.

Jean take a few steps backward then stop and with hacking strokes of the knife make lengthways cuts on her left arm from the back of the hand to the elbow. Then she put the knife in her other hand and do the same to her right arm. As she do this her lips move like she sing or something but no sound come out of her mouth.

We all stopped our walk except Billy who by now handed the baby to Mrs. Winemuller and be on his way back. Rev. Beyer is read from the Bible but his words don't carry this far. Jean's arms be at her side and blood drip from her fingertips into the fine grey dust and onto her running shoes. She toss back the tangled hair from her face and wait for Billy to get back to her.

I look over at Etta. She nod her head to me and make what could be the start of a smile.

goose moon

Because Hector Tree don't speak only a word or two of English, Corporal Greer of the RCMP pick me out to be Hector's translator when they question him at the RCMP office, and then most a year later at the trial for murder in the big new court house in Edmonton.

It was winter, sometime before Christmas they say, when Hector Tree killed Joe Nepoose. Ain't many trappers around anymore but that's what Joe and Hector was. They live what must be close to twenty mile back in the bush. To get there you go until the dirt road ends then walk for maybe half a mile on a winding path that white people would call an Indian trail.

Joe Nepoose got him a wife called Betty and four or five kids. Hector been trapping friends with Joe for ten year or more. He don't live in with Joe but in a hut about 50 yards from Joe's cabin.

They is what we call bush Indians cause they only come to town twice a year. Once to sell their furs and another time to buy food and stuff for the winter. Joe and Betty don't send their kids to school and they live so far from town that nobody want to bother to check them up.

"What are we supposed to do?" Hector Tree say to me as we sit in a room at the RCMP office. The room got a table and a few of them yellow stacking chairs. One old glass ashtray be the only thing on the table.

"The RCMP guys will ask you a question in English, and I'll make the question into Cree for you. You answer in Cree, and I'll make it into English for the RCMP."

"Sound okay to me," Hector say. "You figure they gonna keep me here for long?"

"I don't know much about what you done. Why did you bring the body out? Why didn't you just bury him? If you just said he died in the winter nobody would ever come around to check you up on it."

Hector look at his hands on the table. The table be dark brown but his hands look black against it. His big fingers be rough as spruce bark and covered with scars from skin animals and handle traps.

"What I done was the right thing to do," he say so soft I hardly catch it.

Boy, what an Indian think is right and what a white man take for right sure be two different things.

"Why don't you tell me all what happened before the RCMPs start questions. We don't want to give them any answers that going to make you look bad."

Hector got on jeans and moccasins and a mackinaw of a green colour. He have a package of Vogue tobacco in his front pocket and a package of Zig Zag cigarette papers. All about him Hector have that rotten fruit smell of a people who ain't washed for a long time. Hector is about 35 and have deep lines all over his face, like mud that cracked in the sun. His hair just been let grow and cut off at the shoulder. It be pretty greasy and he rub his big hands through it every time he talk. His eyes are small and black and the white parts be kind of a fawn colour with lots of red lines in them.

"We was all drunked-up on home-brew and I guess I shot Joe. I don't remember."

"How do you know you did it? Maybe somebody else came around."

"There was only the three of us there. Betty don't know how to shoot the rifle and Joe don't do it to himself."

Hector speak soft and fast. Sometimes what he say kind of make the sound of leaves blow in the wind. He have an accent that sound funny to my ear and make his talking real hard to understand.

"He was my friend. I know I don't mean to hurt him none."

"You shouldn't of brought the body in. What you want the RCMP to do, forgive you, or what?"

"I guess so."

"White men got funny laws. You probably gonna get in trouble. Nobody would of known if . . ."

"I would of," Hector say real final like.

The Government give Hector Tree a lawyer name of John Smith. He is tall and thin with a little black moustache and sideburns. Guess he is pretty young for a lawyer cause he don't look much older than me and he is sure nervous when the police and old lawyers are around. John Smith got glasses with silver rims that he take off and on about once a minute and his voice break sometimes when he try to ask questions.

It sure seem funny to me that the Government lawyers, men who supposed to be real smart and I bet been for ten years to all kinds of universities, only ask a half dozen or so questions, and they just repeat them questions over and over like they expect to get different answers each time they ask.

One of the things that make them so uptight is that Hector take so long to bring in the body.

"It was winter. I got to walk my trap lines. After Joe dead I got to walk his too."

"What did you do with his furs?" everybody want to know.

"Sold them. First I bring in the furs. Then I bring in Joe."

"You sold them in your name?"

"Whose I should of sold them in?"

"Did you give Mrs. Nepoose the money from the fur sale?"

"I buy supplies for her and the kids."

The RCMP and lawyer guys all exchange funny looks, make a lot of notes and talk legal words that I don't understand.

John Smith don't do much but put on and take off his glasses. Mostly he agree with the RCMP but once in a while he kind of apologize to everybody and ask a question. After a few hours everybody decide they going to keep Hector in jail and lay a charge of murder on him for kill Joe Nepoose.

"I kept him froze and don't let the animals get at him. That was the right thing. How come they're mad with me?"

"White man think a lot different about time than we do. They think a lot different about everything than we do." I sure feel sorry for Hector. He ain't the kind of man meant to be locked up no place.

"I wait for the Goose Moon to bring him out on the sleigh. Trapping is over by then."

"They figure you should of brought him out right after it happened."

"Who would of walked my trap lines? I come in then, maybe me and Betty and Joe's kids don't eat this fall. Goose Moon was as soon as I could do it."

Indian moons are about the same as white months only they be named for animals and stuff. February is the Eagle Moon, March the Goose Moon, April the Frog Moon and on like that. March named for the goose cause it be when winter start to soften some and the first flights of Canada Geese be seen going north. When an Indian see them geese he know that spring be close. Indian supposed to say to the geese, "*Pimatisiwin petamawin*," which in Cree mean, bring me life. It kind of like they be the first sign of living after the long dead winter.

One fall, when we was kids, me and my friend Frank Fence-post decide to catch us one of them Canada Geese. We get sticks and slats and a couple of pieces of plywood and we nail together a trap. We put it right down at the edge of a big slough in a grain field, prop open the door, put a handful of grain inside, then we go off into the tall grass and wait. In a while the geese fly down to feed and this here great big one waddle right up into the trap. The door bang shut on him and boy do all hell break loose. He can only get his wings about half open but he rock that trap until he tip it over and he get his feet through the bars what be on the bottom and run up the hill and across the stubble field. It look funny as hell see this here box run up the hill. That goose just run until he shake the trap right apart and he fly off over the field. The last piece drop off his foot when he about twenty feet in the air.

In June, Corporal Greer, John Smith, and them Government lawyers take me with them out to Hector's place. They want to talk to Betty Nepoose. They waited until the weather was good to come out here but they is mad at Hector when he wait for good weather to bring Joe's body to them. But then it always seem to be okay for the Government to take a long time to do not much of anything. Guess they figured that with good weather they could drive all the way in to the cabins, but they still have to leave the cars and walk for a good half mile or more.

Corporal Greer be pretty old for an RCMP. He got kind of a grey face and he try never to hurt nobody's feelings, not like the young RCMPs who like to bash around what they call wagon burners. The city lawyers got on suits and businessman shoes and they puff most as loud as Mad Etta when we have to walk up a hill. We also got to cross a creek that be a foot or two deep. John Smith take off his shoes and socks and wade over, Corporal Greer and the fattest Government lawyer try to hop across on rocks. The fat lawyer get his feet wet and his shoes make slurp sounds the rest of the way.

Betty's cabin built right in among tall spruce, white poplar and balm trees that have big sticky leaves and scatter a kind of white cotton all over. The cabin be built of log and have a sod roof that got pigweed and raspberry canes grow out of it. Fifty yards or so away is a kind of three-cornered cabin with no window and a stove-pipe stick out of the side, that I guess is where Hector lived. Weeds be tall in front of the door of that one.

After us coming from the sunlight the cabin look dark as a cellar. We don't go inside but stand in a group around the door. Betty be 40 or so and don't be what anybody would say is pretty. She be a little bit stooped over with skin black as harness leather. She be really shy with white folks. She probably not been to town more than a dozen time in her life. She whisper worse than Hector when she talk and hardly say more than yes or no to the questions that is asked to her.

"She don't remember nothing," I tell them after they ask Betty about ten times what happened the day Joe got killed.

"What about the children?" one of the lawyer men asks. There be a naked boy play on the dirt floor behind Betty and I can hear other kids inside but can't see them. Betty Nepoose sure look pregnant to me, but then lots of Indian ladies by her age get a little tummy, so maybe not, too.

"We put the kids over to Hector's," she say.

"Why?" the lawyers all want to know.

"So we could have us a good drunk. Joe and Hector been cooking up potato wine for a month or so." I translate that so she say she put the kids away so they won't see the big people drunk. I figure it sound better. Even when I put it that way the lawyers all look at each other like they just heard some swear words.

"Did Hector always live over there?"

"Sure," say Betty.

"After Joe was dead, where did he live?"

"Over here," and Betty shrug her shoulder.

"Why?" the fat lawyers say again.

"Why not?" say Betty. "My man was dead."

Corporal Greer and the lawyers, even John Smith, all look like somebody just swung a skunk through our crowd. All the way back to town they give each other secret looks and click their tongues like a grandmother who just found out her son-in-law is the bad bugger she always suspect he was.

Along about August, there be in the court house in Edmonton, what called a Preliminary Hearing. Seem pretty much like a trial to me. Everybody tell their story and the judge have to decide if there going to be a real for sure murder trial. It get held up for a couple of days when Betty Nepoose don't show up like she supposed to. One of them sheriff guys from the court house say that he serve the papers himself to tell her she got to come to court on a certain day. I have to explain that Betty don't read neither English or Cree, so having papers delivered on her don't mean much.

I get to go along when they go and get her. She just shrug her shoulder and come along. I had to get the sheriff to stop at Hobbema and we get Connie Bigcharles to come stay with Betty's kids. Sheriff never thought of that, guess he figure it okay to leave the Indian kids alone.

"Are you with child?" is one of the questions that the Government lawyer ask Betty.

I'm pretty sure he mean pregnant but I call John Smith over and get him to tell me for sure, not that there be any doubt about it now, at least to my eye.

"Yes," Betty says.

"When are you due?"

Betty shrug her shoulder to me.

"When did you bleed last?" I ask her.

"What do they care for?"

"White men are crazy." After I say that is about the first time I ever seen Betty smile.

"The time of the Great Moon," she say.

"She had her last period in January," I tell them.

"What were you talking about with her?" one lawyer say to me.

"I was explain your questions."

"Are you sure you're not telling her how to answer? Ask her whose baby it is."

"Joe Nepoose died in November. What more do you want to hear?"

"Ask her anyway."

Mr. John Smith take off his glasses and make some objection and after they argue for an hour or so they never get back to the question. Finally, after everybody finish arguing with everybody else, the judge say that Hector Tree got to have a real trial.

It be March again before that come up in what they call the Supreme Court of Alberta. Hector's got pale and his hands be smoothed out so they look like black gloves. I talk to my friend Dave Smallface at the Indian Friendship Centre and he go to the Salvation Army and get for Hector a suit to wear at his trial. The suit be old and dark blue and it don't fit right. It make Hector look small and scared, and he ain't neither of them.

"It's the Goose Moon, right?" Hector say to me during one of the breaks in the trial. As he do it he give me kind of a shy smile.

"Right," I say back to him.

"I keep track in my head. If I could get outside I could smell the air and tell you what moon it is."

About the only difference between the real trial and the Preliminary Hearing is that there is a jury at the trial. The lawyers go through all the same stuff as they did before. Whole thing be kind of like a medicine ceremony of some kind. The lawyers make a big deal of Hector moving in with Betty, and of him selling the furs off Joe's trap line. They bring in the bill of sale Hector got for the furs and wave it around like it be a skeleton or something.

All that stuff put together be what is called a motive, so John Smith tell me. Lawyers just don't understand about how life really is. But then neither do Hector or he would of kept himself quiet.

After I tell John Smith about Mad Etta our medicine

lady, he get me to arrange for her to come to court to tell that Hector Tree have a good character. The jury made up mostly of old white ladies with blue hair, and they giggle some when Etta waddle into the court dressed up in her five-flour-sack dress with fox tails pinned down both sleeves. Etta be too broad across the back to sit in the witness chair so she have to do her talk while she stand up.

I get to translate for Etta too. Even though she can speak as good English as I can she say she rather talk in Cree. Etta don't speak to the court, she speak to me and by the tone of her voice I know I better listen pretty good.

"Tell these dumb buggers," she say to me in Cree, "that Hector Tree probably done what he said he done—things like that happen when everybody go on a drunk. He don't do it for Joe's woman or Joe's furs. It just happen. And if they got half the brains of a dead muskrat they let him go back so's he can look after Betty and her kids."

I soften up her language quite a bit when I translate. Don't figure it do any good to rile up these white people on the jury.

Betty bring her newest baby to the courtroom and she hold it up for Hector to see. He make the better part of a smile when she do that.

That day at lunch John Smith tell me that this is his first-ever murder trial and that he don't know for sure what he should say to try to make things easy for Hector.

Only thing I can think to tell him is that he should make sure the jury know that Hector and Joe and Betty, they pay their own way by trapping and hunting. Don't even cost the Government money for school on the kids. White folks is always complain about all the money they is spend on us Indians.

"Tell them, if they send Hector to jail, they not only got to pay for keep him there, but I personal get somebody to show Betty how to get on the welfare. With all the kids she got she be able to get more than they ever made on trapping. If they let Hector go it save everybody money. Hector shouldn't of killed Joe, but it done, and no use mess up everybody because of it."

I figure lawyers and maybe even the jury would go for something like that, that save money. Lawyers sure like money. One I went to see in Edmonton once, charge me 50 dollars in advance just to tell me he couldn't be of no help.

The trial only last for a day and a half. The last afternoon, John Smith read from the Bible, something about mercy and stuff. The old ladies scratch their blue heads and wrinkle up their noses when they look at Hector.

I am leaning on the wall by the water fountain when the court man come and say that the jury coming back. The courtroom is most empty as I go in. The windows be maybe 40 feet tall and got on them up and down gold bars for the first fifteen feet or so, bars that look like ones on teller's cages at the old Bank of Montreal in Wetaskiwin.

"All rise," the court man say, and the judge come up from behind his bench and sit down.

"Have you reached a verdict?" the judge say to the jury.

The guy on one corner of the jury box, the only man on the whole jury, stand up and say, "We have, your honour." Then he go on to say that they found the defendant guilty of murder. I check with John Smith to make sure that Hector was the defendant. I didn't really think they could find somebody else guilty but I thought it was worth a try.

"They found you guilty," I tell Hector.

"Of what?" he says.

"Of killing Joe."

"I know that. What they gonna do about it?"

"Wait for a minute," I tell him. "The judge is gonna say something."

No use my repeat what the judge say. It mainly be about how he agree with the jury and how Hector sure be one bad character for what he done.

"What's he saying?"

"He telling what a bad bugger you are. They found you guilty of moving in with Betty more than anything else."

"I done what was right," Hector say and make kind of a

small laugh.

The judge ask Hector if he have anything to say before he pass sentence.

"You think it would help if I cry?" Hector say to me. "I was up on a drunk charge one time and the white guy in front of me cried and got let go. I don't say nothing and got 21 days."

"He don't have nothing to say," I tell the judge.

He sentence Hector to life in prison.

Hector be looking out them tall windows where the sky is grey and a cold wind blow, though there ain't no snow on the ground.

"You got to go back to jail," I tell him.

"For a long time?"

"For a long time." I can't make myself say life in prison to him.

"I'm gone soft as a woman," he say and show me his big, soft hands. "I need to be out in the sun. I don't live . . ."

All this time he never once look at me. His eyes be staring out them tall windows. I don't know if Hector see something up there that I don't, but he just keep lean forward on the shiny wood rail of the prisoner's box. It when a policeman put a hand on him to take him back to jail that Hector move fast as a cat. He push over that policeman, put one big hand on the rail, vault over, take a dozen steps and jump up to catch a hold of the long gold bars on the window.

The judge stand up in his chair and the few people in the court gasp in their breath. Hector climb as high as he can go on the bars and just hang there.

"*Pimatisiwin petamawin*," he shout out a few times at the sky outside the window.

It take five or six of them RCMP guys in their brown uniforms to finally pull him down.

the four-sky-thunder bundle

Calgary Stampede come up every July. Bunch of us decide to go this summer but a whole lot more end up than we really planned on. Start out just me and my girlfriend Sadie One-wound, my friend Frank Fence-post and his girl Connie Bigcharles. We was gonna borrow Blind Louis Coyote's pickup truck and drive down for a day or so. Then Blind Louis decide that he never seen the Stampede so he'd like to go. We pretty well have to take him cause it be his truck. Then the Glenbow Institute in Calgary ask Solomon Stiff-arm to loan them the Four-Sky-Thunder bundle to display in the Indian exhibits, so when Solomon ask to ride along we can hardly say no. By the day we ready to go it seem that about half the reserve hang around our cabin. We have to decide who sit in the cab and who ride behind.

First we take the door off One-wound's outhouse, use it

for a ramp to load Mad Etta our medicine lady in the back of the truck. Etta she weigh so much she fill up the cab all by herself if we was even able to stuff all of her in there. Second, we load up the ramp and put Etta's chair up in the truck for her to sit on.

I drive. My girl Sadie sit close beside me. Then come Blind Louis who hold on to his cane with both hands. He got white hair to his shoulders and eyes the colour of skim milk. Then there is my ma who sit with Delores my littlest sister on her knee. About this time Mrs. Blind Louis decide she going to go too. My hip is already pushed up hard against the door and I have to bend my arm funny to reach the gearshift. When I open the door the push of all the people spring me right out of the truck.

I fit in Mrs. Blind Louis Coyote where Sadie used to be. Sadie make a face at me cause she have to sit in the back and she say she wish we never told nobody we was going.

Mrs. Blind Louis is heavy with her next baby and her and Louis argue most of the way to Red Deer if it be sixteen or seventeen. Nobody win that argument.

That make five of us in the cab, not count the baby. In the back is:

Mad Etta on her tree-trunk chair, her tarpaulin over her head like about a size-100 parka.

My girlfriend Sadie One-wound.

My friend Frank Fence-post who's brought along a sleeping bag cause he figure him an Connie was gonna be alone back there in the truck box.

Connie Bigcharles.

Rufus Firstrider.

Rufus' white girlfriend Winnie Bear who been sick a lot. She sit close to Rufus, hug his arm and say she hope they don't get lost in Calgary.

Mrs. Chief Tom Crow-eye all decked up in her chicken-dancer costume.

My brother Joseph, who be big, strong, older than me but have only a little kid's mind. He jump up and down like a puppy need to be petted and make sounds like the birds he hear sing around the reserve.

Eathen Firstrider, my big sister's old boyfriend. Eathen got on his red-and-white cowhide chaps, and a cowboy hat have leather thongs hang down all the way around it. Eathen is quite a bit over six feet tall.

Eathen's new girlfriend, Julie Scar.

Julie's brother Norman.

Solomon Stiffarm hanging on tight to the Four-Sky-Thunder bundle.

Norman Scar's friend Eddy Wolfchild.

Eddy's girlfriend Blanche Powder.

A couple of guys I seen around the reserve but don't know the name of.

Have to drive pretty slow down the corduroy road to Hobbema and the highway. The truck ain't got much in the way of shocks or springs or stuff like that. We stop for gas at the Hobbema Texaco Garage and they tell us that Robert Coyote just phoned up to say he got let out of jail down at Drumheller. He been away for about seven months for have stolen stuff around his place. The garageman, Fred Crier, say he told Robert that me and Frank was going to the Stampede and that Robert says he'll hitch-hike to Highway 2 and that we're to wait for him at the crossroads. He also say we should bring along his girlfriend Bertha Bigcharles and a blanket.

Robert is our friend but he is also about the toughest dude around the reserve. What Robert say we is all pretty quick to do. If we have to wait at the crossroads for a couple of days we will. First though we go back up the hill to our cabins and get Bertha Bigcharles. Bertha she be in the same shape as Mrs. Blind Louis and she figure that sure be a nice surprise for Robert when she see him.

When we get to Drumheller crossroad Robert he is already there. He sure surprised to see so many peoples in the truck and to see the way Bertha is built when she stand up and lean over the side to kiss him.

We stop off for a few beers at a town south of Red Deer. Must be a reserve close by cause there be two white farmers and about 50 Indians in the beer parlour.

It wasn't us that started the fight. These here Indians figure they is about the toughest guys around. Couple of them try to stare us down but we look right back at them. A big tall dude with a headband, denim vest, and one front tooth missing, come over to our table. He say he hear there be a whole lot of cowards live up at the Ermineskin Reserve at Hobbema, right after he ask us where we come from and we told him. Robert Coyote start to get up but Bertha pull him down again, and Mad Etta got a hold of Frank and Eathen by one arm each, keep them in their chairs.

That dude walk slow back to his table and the whole bunch of them have a good laugh at us.

"We'd of killed them," say Frank, bounce up and down some on his chair.

"No use fighting unless you got a chance to win," say Etta.

That dude come back to our table and this time he got a couple of guys on each side of him.

"We hear you Crees sell your women," he say. Then he toss two pennies on the table and reach out his hand for Julie Scar.

His hand get within about two inches of Julie's arm when Eathen Firstrider's fist hit on his chin, and back he go half-way across the bar, take out a table that have a white farmer on each side of it. Them white guys just sit and look at each other over the space where their table used to be. The Indian and the table be in a heap against the wall.

After that everybody is fight with everybody else. There must be twice as many of them as us so I don't get to see all that goes on cause a short dude in a red flannel shirt is busy try to break my ribs with his fists.

I do see Mrs. Coyote point Blind Louis at where them strange Indians is. She talk into his ear, tell him where to hit with his white cane. Once he whack across the shoulders that dude who is pounding on me. The guy yell and look up to see what happening and it give me a chance to let my right fist make his nose some flatter than it was before.

Robert and Eathen be back to back in the centre of the room their fists going like buzz saws. They got around them a little pile of guys that got too close.

Sadie and Julie be kicking at a couple of dudes that got Frank Fence-post on the floor and pounding on him pretty good. I see Mad Etta draw back her big right leg that look like the trunk of a real old spruce tree and kick the ribs of a guy who be sitting on and beating on Norman Scar. It sound like she kicking a piece of plywood when she thump him.

Joseph sit and smile and shake happy at all the excitement until a big Indian in bib overalls raise up his fist to Ma. Joseph grab that guy and shake him back and forth the way a dog shake a groundhog.

It is about this time that the RCMP get in on the fight. Five or six of them come through the door of the bar and start to haul guys off one another. A constable so big he look like he wear football pads under his uniform, lift up the dude I fight with and slam him against the wall. In a minute, instead of fight each other, us Indians fight the RCMP. We would of won too but another eight-ten RCMPs break in and soon everything is quiet and the waiters creep out from behind the bar, walk soft like maybe they in a hospital, and start to push around mops and brooms to clean up the glass and beer.

The RCMP load us all up in our truck. Even a couple of them help push Mad Etta up the ramp. Joseph still be shaking that Indian in bib overalls and it take me and Ma and about seven RCMP to make him let go.

The big dude who started the fight, his name be Leonard Redrock, say to Eathen as the RCMP load us up in the truck, "Hey, partner, that was some good fight. Be sure and stop in on your way back from Calgary. We give you a chance to get even."

Everybody laugh some except the RCMP guys who groan and tell us they don't ever want to see us in town again.

"If you ever come up our way," say Frank Fence-post, "we ain't got no hotel at Hobbema, but we fight you at the bar of the Alice Hotel in Wetaskiwin."

"We remember," say Leonard Redrock, who now got one less tooth in the front of his face than he had when the fight started. Sirens going, the RCMP drive, one car in front, one car behind, until we get to the highway.

It already dark when we get to Calgary. We stop at the first liquor store we see and most everybody buy up at least one case of Lethbridge Pale Ale. We know we never gonna get no hotel to stay at during Stampede week, so we figure to stay with my sister Illianna and her husband. They live in a fancy apartment on the fourteenth floor of a big building right downtown. Illianna is married to a white man, and he is not the type that is gonna be very excited to see us drop in for a visit.

The big glass thing with the buttons at the front of the apartment say Mr. & Mrs. Robert M. McVey for number 1410. While the others are unloading Mad Etta from the truck, me and Sadie, Ma, Joseph and Delores, ring the bell.

"Hello," say the voice of my brother-in-law.

"Tell him to let us in," says Ma.

"You tell him," I say, "just talk into the machine."

"This here's Suzie Ermineskin. I come to see my girl."

"What a nice surprise," say Robert McGregor McVey. "Come on up," and there is a snap sound to let us know the door is unlocked.

I hold the door open and everybody run whooping for the elevators. This building got a lobby with thick red carpet and a marble pool with goldfish float in it. Somebody push Frank a little bit and he step one foot on the goldfish on the way across. There be two elevators and when the first one open everybody is shove inside. Frank and Connie push all seventeen buttons and the others yell at them for doing it.

We wait for the second one: Sadie, Ma, Delores, Mad Etta and Joseph carrying Etta's chair.

"Etta should have an elevator all for herself," she say and laugh and laugh.

Illianna and Brother Bob have their door open when we get off.

"Come in. Come in," say Brother Bob. Illianna hugs Ma. Joseph and Delores kind of make strange. Brother Bob's eyes get big when he see the size of Mad Etta who got to turn sideways to get through the door. His eyes damn near fall out of his face when the other elevator open and them sixteen or so Indians come charging out.

Doors open all up and down the hall because of all the noise.

"Why do you hate me?" Brother Bob say, looking right at me.

Robert McVey is shorter than Illianna. He have pink cheeks and light brown hair that he have in a crew cut, the only one in Calgary, I bet. Even around his apartment he wear his suit, with a vest, and businessman shoes. When he go out he wear a funny little hat with no brim. Me and Frank make jokes that he probably wear that suit and shoes to bed. Illianna say that he treat her nice and that he don't drink a lot or be mean to her, and that we shouldn't make fun on him just for being white. But Brother Bob don't know how to act around Indians and I guess we don't know how to act around white peoples, so when we get together there always be plenty of trouble.

All of a sudden Brother Bob spot Frank.

"No way that Post-hole fellow is coming in my house," he say.

"Fence-post," says Frank.

"Whatever," say my brother-in-law. "Si I've got to put up with cause he's my wife's brother, but that Post-hole guy pushed me in a creek, stole my baby, got me arrested . . ."

"Don't worry," say Frank. "I just mix in with the crowd. You never know I'm here," and he push into the apartment pulling Connie Bigcharles along by the hand.

All of us sit around on the furniture and the floor. Everybody got a beer and feeling pretty happy, except Brother Bob. Illianna bring out their baby, Bobby, and Ma get to hold on to her grandson for the first time. Joseph sit in the corner making bird calls, which is what he do good, and Brother Bob jump about a foot everytime he do his meadowlark.

Illianna come and whisper to me, say she hope we don't all plan on staying the night.

"Don't worry," I tell her. "We try real hard not to make Brother Bob mad."

Julie Scar gone through their records and put on a Linda Ronstadt album on the record player. I think Robert Coyote and Bertha Bigcharles gone to the bedroom. After all, Robert been away for seven months.

Frank pull back the curtains and look out at the view of the city. "Boy, this is about as close to heaven as any of us ever gonna get," he say.

"Amen to that," say Robert McVey.

There be what Illianna say is French doors that go out on to a balcony. Frank open them up and take him, the sleeping bag, and Connie Bigcharles out with him. When Frank stretch and start to take off his shirt I run over quick and close up the curtains.

Louis Coyote bang his cane on the coffee table and say that he's hungry. Also, he want to know where the hell he is. He say he don't hear no chuckwagons racing so this can't be the Stampede. Mrs. Blind Louis sit with her legs spread way out the way pregnant ladies do.

Little Bobby is walk and talk some by now, and it sure funny, but the first person he walk to, after Illianna put him down on the floor, is Eathen Firstrider. We all know that Eathen be the baby's real daddy, and we all sure proud that Illianna have a full-time Indian baby.

Eathen bounce Bobby on his knee and Bobby sure like the pearl buttons on Eathen's shirt.

Brother Bob is busy run around with ashtrays. All us Indians except Joseph and Delores, smoke. A job like that is keep him pretty busy. Illianna tell us that they bought themselves a house on the North side of town with four bedrooms and a big back yard.

"With four bedrooms a couple of dozen of us be able to move in permanent," I say. Brother Bob turn pale cause he never been one to know a joke when he hear one.

After a while the music get louder and the party kind of spill out into the hall.

"Why don't somebody get us some food?" say Blind Louis. He hit the coffee table again and tip over a bottle of beer.

"Let's all go someplace for Chinese food," say Rufus.

"Why don't we phone out for food and have it delivered?" say Rufus' girlfriend, Winnie Bear, who used to live in the city.

"Why don't you all go out for food?" says Brother Bob.

We pool up our money and order up about $70 worth of Chinese food. Right after we do that the phone ring and after Brother Bob talk for a while he stand up on the coffee table and tell us to be quiet cause that was the caretaker telling him that we make too much noise.

Blind Louis say that it sound like a white man talking and he slap the table again with his cane and hit Brother Bob on the toes.

I guess Joseph he never been anywhere to hear a phone ring before. He sure like it and he make the sound exactly like he hear it. Brother Bob run quick to answer the phone again and we all have a good laugh while Joseph grin happy and shake up and down some.

After a while the food come.

"Taste like something out of the slop bucket," say Blind Louis. "How come we don't get no meat? I want meat!"

Mrs. Blind Louis pop a pineapple chicken ball in his mouth, tell him to shut up.

The music get loud again. Rufus go out to the truck for his tom-tom and Mrs. Chief Tom Crow-eye do her famous chicken dance. She don't dance good but she is a nice lady and nobody want to hurt her feelings by telling her. Somebody open up the door and Mrs. Chief Tom dance up and down the hall some. People open up their doors and yell for us to be quiet cause they want to get some sleep.

"You get as much sleep as you want, you don't bother us none," Rufus tell them.

Joseph he make lots of telephone sounds.

Then there appear a little man with a bald head, round gold glasses and a bathrobe that be striped red and white like a candy cane.

"I'm going to have to call the police if this party isn't toned down immediately," he say.

"When you call the police tell them to bring along a few cases of beer, we're running short," Eathen Firstrider says to him. The little man's face get as red as his dressing gown.

"I am a retired RCMP officer and I will not take this."

"Take it easy, Corporal Travis," Brother Bob say. "I'll get them to quiet down. They're my wife's relatives. I had no idea there were so many of them or I never would have let them in."

Then Brother Bob go and unplug the record player. He take away Rufus' drum and hand it to Solomon Stiffarm who been sit in the corner all night not say a word, and he point his finger at Ma tell her to stop Joseph from make any more telephone ringing sounds.

After Brother Bob get everybody back into the apartment and the door closed, the little corporal go away. "Police brutality," we all say after him, and some of us give the clenched-fist Red Power salute.

We pass around the last of the beer and Solomon Stiffarm unwrap the Four-Sky-Thunder bundle at the same time as he hold on to Rufus' drum. Solomon Stiffarm be about 50, he got a long sad face, two black braids that touch his shoulders, a buckskin jacket and pants with fringes, and a back as straight as a broom handle. He hold on to the things from the Four-Sky-Thunder bundle with his long slim fingers the colour of red willow.

"*Ah sas soo wayo*," he say, which in Cree mean tattooing.

He tell us how long time ago when both Cree men and women had tattoos, Four-Sky-Thunder was the master tattoo man in all the West. His tattooing bundle be passed down from generation to generation. Solomon say that them museum people want to keep it but that he just loan it to them for special occasion like the Stampede exhibits.

Inside the bundle are a bag of red willow charcoal, a stick

decorated with split owl feathers that be used to make the outline of the tattoo with some charcoal and water what been mixed up in a dish. Then there is eight steel needles: in the real old days they used porcupine quills. These be tied together by a thong and tied to a stick got on it hawk bells that rattle and keep down the noise of the person being tattooed.

It been a whole lot of years since Indians got tattooed this way, Solomon explain. Used to be young men had their chests and arms tattooed this way to show how brave they are, and the women have lines from their mouth to their chin to show off how beautiful they are.

Then he show us a buffalo-skin mask that the tattooist wear, and he demonstrate to us how the tattoo man blot up the blood with this here mask which be real scary looking. Then Solomon mix some beer and charcoal in a bottle cap and draw on the face of Rufus' drum a picture he say is called Buffalo That Walks Like A Man. He say if he is really tattooing he poke holes in the skin with the needles and then use the other stick to mix in the colour, then blot the whole thing with his mask.

Eathen, Rufus and Eddy Wolfchild all say they'd like to get tattooed some. Eathen got on his chest an eagle with green claws that he got done in Edmonton by a Gypsy man named Pico the Rat. "No!" say Solomon Stiffarm. Indian tattooing have religious meaning and not just anybody could get tattooed. It take hours and hours to do and just be part of our past now, but he say he learning his son, Jerry Stiffarm, to do tattoos on rabbit skin just in case it ever come back.

By now it maybe three in the morning and everybody is calm and get sleepy. Delores gone to sleep on Joseph's knee. Mad Etta lean back in her tree-trunk chair and snore like the six o'clock CPR train that go through Hobbema.

Brother Bob kick Robert and Bertha out of his bedroom, and him, Illianna and Bobby go to bed. I find me and Sadie a spot on the thick carpet behind the sofa, and we cuddle up close. We let Mr. and Mrs. Blind Louis sleep on the sofa. Louis he take off his wooden leg that been bought for him by the Department of Indian Affairs. He take off that wooden leg when he sleep and lay it behind the sofa where me and Sadie is. For some reason Sadie think it real funny that Blind Louis' leg is watch us and she giggle into my shoulder for a real long time.

While I sleeping I seem to dream of somebody making gun shots and of people cheering. Then the phone ring real loud right in my ear. I sure hope it ain't Joseph. I look at the clock on Brother Bob's wall and it say seven o'clock, and it is the real phone that is ringing. Somebody took it off the table and set it down near my head.

"Hello," I say.

"Mr. McVey, this is Corporal Travis. We have a report that there are Indians...ah...fornicating on your balcony."

"Not here," I say. "Must be one flight up or one flight down. Ain't no Indians here."

"Is that Mr. McVey?"

"I'm a friend of his."

"You're an Indian. I can tell by your voice."

"Who is it?" say Brother Bob. He stand rub sleep from his face. He wears a blue-and-white-striped night shirt make him look like a lady.

I hand the phone to Brother Bob. Then I go over and pull back the curtains. That guy ain't wrong. Connie got her legs wrapped tight around Frank and I sure hope they ain't gonna shake that balcony off the building. I open the French door just a little. What I dreamed was gun shots is my fault. Last night I tried to clean up a little for Illianna and I must of put about 50 beer bottles out on the balcony. Now Frank and Connie bouncing around is shaking them off the edge of the balcony and when they hit the parking lot way down below they sound like gun shots.

There is another apartment building straight across the parking lot from us and people there be out on their balconies look over here at Frank and Connie.

"Way to go fella," someone yell.

"Atta boy," say someone else. Lots of them people got binoculars. Some others don't say nothing but just clap their hands. I bang on the glass to get Frank's attention, but he just wave his hand to say hello and keep right on with what he is doing.

Brother Bob be busy apologize into the telephone. By the time he hang up his face be redder than any of ours. He quick pick off the floor a blanket, push me out of the way, open up the glass doors and cover up Frank's back. Then he pull what left of the bottles away from the balcony edge.

"Boo," yell the peoples from across the way.

It be just about then that Mrs. Blind Louis start having her bad pains. Brother Bob go for the phone again say that he call up an ambulance. Blind Louis, his wife, Sadie, Ma and Mad Etta hold council in Cree around the sofa.

Bobby come from the bedroom in yellow pyjamas, eat from a box of Fruit Loops and pull a wooden duck on a string. He go straight to Eathen Firstrider and bounce on Eathen's stomach.

"Mrs. Coyote say nobody but Mad Etta can deliver her baby," Sadie tell us.

"She done the other seventeen," say Blind Louis, "why should we change now?"

"Sixteen," say Mrs. Edith Coyote, between pains.

"You mean she's going to have it here?" yell Brother Bob.

"Why not?" say Etta. "You never seen a baby born before? Nothing to it."

Brother Bob bash his fist on his forehead.

"You want me to boil some water?" he say.

"Sure," say Mad Etta. "When it boiling good you put a couple of rabbits in it, then you drink the soup. It keep you calm."

We all have a good laugh about that.

Every little while Mrs. Blind Louis give out a good loud yell. People bang on the door, say, "Knock off the noise in there."

Robert Coyote open the door tell them we having a baby in here and that he take a couple of scalps if they don't go away. Illianna make some coffee but she only got eight cups so we pass them around the room let everybody get a taste or two.

The baby come with not much trouble at all. Only thing loses out is the white sofa. Illianna give Mrs. Coyote some of Bobby's baby clothes and a blanket.

"Where is this place anyway?" say Blind Louis.

"Robert McVey's house," say Frank. "He's the guy married Illianna Ermineskin."

Blind Louis rub his hand on his chin.

"We already got a Robert," he say. "McVey's a stupid name, but I guess we call the baby that anyway."

"You could call him Seventeen," suggest Frank.

"Sixteen," say Mrs. Blind Louis.

One time old Davis Rattlesnake named his son Noon, after the time of day he was born. Everyone joke that the next baby be called Afternoon. But it was a girl and they named it Belinda.

"McVey Coyote, you hear that Brother Bob," I say.

Brother Bob just stand in the middle of the room in his nightgown, look like a steer been hit between the eyes with a sledgehammer.

"How are *you* feeling?" Blind Louis say to Bertha Big-charles, and he put his old brown hand on her belly where it bulge out over the top of her jeans. "Maybe I get to be a father and grandfather on the same day. Not bad for be over 80 years old," and he wrinkle up his face, laugh and whack his cane on the coffee table.

Some of the guys gone out to the store and come back with cigars for everybody. The air get so thick we can hardly see one another. Then there come to the door that Corporal Travis guy, only now he dressed up in a suit like Brother Bob wear. He take one breath of the apartment and cough for a while. Then he hand Brother Bob a white paper say it be his eviction notice. They got to clear out of the apartment by the end of July.

"You can't do that," Brother Bob say. "Our house won't be ready until October. Where are we going to go for three months?"

"Far away, I hope," says Corporal Travis. "You've caused more trouble in the last twelve hours than the rest of my tenants have in a year."

"Illianna and Bobby can come live with me," say Mad Etta. "You can write them a letter every month or so see how they doing."

"If you don't have these Indians out of here in fifteen minutes I'll call the police," say Corporal Travis.

All of a sudden Brother Bob let out a howl like a dog that got its tail caught in a cabin door. He pick up the phone and when he get his number say, "Send the police," and he give his address. "There's a riot here and there will be about 50 dead Indians if you don't hurry."

"There not even 25 of us," say Frank. "We just seem like 50."

"He's not a very good host," Blind Louis say in Cree, and poke his cane in the direction of Brother Bob's voice. Only he poke the cane hard into the back of Brother Bob's nightshirt. Brother Bob whirl around, grab the cane away, and bust it over his knee.

"Ooooh!" says everybody.

We all start to gather up our stuff. A couple of us guys help Mrs. Blind Louis. The police must of been close cause half a dozen or so of them come run off the elevator just as some of our people is getting on.

"Get them all out of here," Brother Bob yell, and he push and shove people toward the door.

A cop start herding Illianna and Bobby along with us.

"Not them, they're mine," Brother Bob say and take hold on Illianna's arm. Bobby is crying cause he don't want Eathen Firstrider to put him down.

Mad Etta is have trouble wiggle her way through the door. Brother Bob put the flat of his foot against her big back and push her out into the hall.

Mad Etta rumble some at him in Cree. My brother-in-law also give a hard push to Solomon Stiffarm, knock loose the Four-Sky-Thunder bundle and Solomon have to kneel down in the hall to pick up the pieces.

We all spend the day downtown. Seeing as Illianna is our sister we figure we should try to make peace so we buy a pair of cowboy boots for Bobby and send them over in a taxi. About supper time I phone Illianna, ask if her and Bobby like to go to the Stampede, and say that I come for her all by myself. She guesses it would be okay.

"I don't suppose Brother Bob would want to come too," I say.

Illianna say she don't suppose he would.

When I get to the apartment Illianna answer the talk-back machine and say come on up. She got Bobby dressed up in yellow overalls, a cowboy hat and the boots we bought for him. Brother Bob be reading the want-ads in the newspaper and he pretend that I am not there even when I say hello to him and wave my hand a little bit.

In the elevator Illianna say that he's pretty mad about them having to move out of the apartment before their new house is ready. As we go out the front door, I stick in between the lock and the door a sponge that I bought for fifteen cents at the Metropolitan Store.

As we walk to the truck I see Mad Etta's buffalo-big shadow at the corner of the building, and as we drive away I can see in the rear-view mirror Etta, Robert, Eathen, Rufus and Solomon Stiffarm, head for the door I left open. Under Solomon Stiffarm's right arm be the Four-Sky-Thunder bundle.

fawn

"Silas, now that you is learning Mad Etta's secrets you got to help me make Winnie Bear all better."

That be my friend Rufus Firstrider talking. And Winnie Bear is his girlfriend. They live in a cabin Rufus built up on the hill about a quarter of a mile from our place.

Winnie Bear, in spite of have what sure sound like an Indian name, be a white girl. Girls don't come no whiter than Winnie Bear. She be really tall and slim and have long blond hair the colour of a lemon milkshake. I heard her real name one time, but I forgot it. She call herself Winnie Bear after somebody in a story her daddy read to her when she was little. She pronounce her name like it was one word. It be a name that she take when she first come visit us for the summer with my cousin Pauline.

"You know Mad Etta say she won't help Winnie Bear

no more. But I figure you can do it, Silas."

Just a while ago, Mad Etta say to me that she like for me to be her assistant, and that she'll learn me all the secrets of be a doctor.

"I ain't done nothing so far but help Mad Etta make up a couple of medicine bags," I tell Rufus, who is twenty years old and a real close friend to me, so I sure would help him if I could.

Rufus sure do love Winnie Bear. In one way I am real happy for him and in another I am real sad. Winnie Bear been awful sick ever since she took some bad drugs of some kind when she still live in the city. She don't be like a girl who is eighteen, she be more like my littlest sister, Delores, who is almost seven.

As Rufus and me is walk along and talk we take turns carrying a fawn we found. We was on our way out to cut some poplar logs make a wall for a wood shed Rufus be building when we all of a sudden scare off a fawn and its mother. As it run away the fawn step in a hole in the ground and I can hear its leg break as it falls. It be pretty scared, heart beating like the exhaust on a trail bike, but me and Rufus carry it back toward our cabins. We can't figure what to do with it except to take it to Mad Etta.

Etta be sitting in her cabin on her tree-trunk chair.

"You bringing me a four-legged Indian?" she say and laugh and laugh, shake all over like a big sack of potatoes.

"It got a broke leg," Rufus say. "We figure you could fix it."

Rufus is small and got kind of a pinched face. His eyes be real close together and his hair grow out in all directions and fall all the time over his eyes, but like they say about some people, he got a good heart.

Rufus still believe that Mad Etta could make his girl-friend good as new if she really wanted to. She did help her some and he be grateful for that but it don't stop him from keep asking for more help.

Winnie Bear wasn't always as good as she is now. When Pauline bring her back from the city to keep the Welfare from put her in the crazy place, she don't be able to talk or nothing and Rufus and me have to feed her by pry open her mouth and poke food inside.

Mad Etta was away someplace when Pauline brought Winnie Bear home and for a week or so we kept her at our place and Rufus and me feed her and wash her face. Rufus he comb her hair real gentle and try put on her face some of the pretty things she liked, like blue eye shadow and orange lipstick. We sure be glad to see Etta come back and we ask her quick fix up Winnie Bear and make her better again. Pauline say Winnie been showed to a bunch of white doctors and they say there ain't nothing can be done for her. But we all know that Etta be better than white-man doctors, why one time she brew medicine that cause my sister Illianna make a baby even though she been taking them birth control pills.

From about the time they was twelve Pauline and Winnie Bear spend their summers on the reserve, and Winnie and Rufus sort of been promised to each other, though I wonder sometimes if a white girl know what it mean to be promised to somebody. Winnie be a funny kind of girl, so smart in school, Pauline say, that she be a couple of grades ahead of where she should be. But Winnie don't get along with her mother, and her daddy he live way off in the east somewhere. That mother be glad to get rid of Winnie for the summers, she say Winnie be crazy like Indians she should go live with them. At least that's what Pauline tell us.

People around the reserve who don't know Winnie, call her the Butterfly Girl, cause she like to chase butterflies. She sure look funny, all tall and wobbly-kneed, run across the hills chase those brown, white and yellow butterflies with a net made from a pair of my mother's old panties. She fall down lots of times but get up look quick at her scrapes and keep on going.

Etta make me go down to the muskeg get a bucket of green moss, while she boil up a bunch of roots and bark and stuff in a saucepan on her wood stove. She send Rufus out to get two long pieces of wood for make splints. Then she hold a medicine bag, smell like burning egg shells, against the fawn's nose and pretty soon it go to sleep. First she wrap the broken leg in moss, put a board on each side, then wrap it up tight with pieces of an old shirt of mine that been soaked in the stuff she cook on the stove. Stuff that be thick and black and look like an oil change down to the Texaco Garage at Hobbema.

It remind me some of the way she used to doctor Winnie Bear. She cut off the hair on the top of her head and rub on what she say be bear grease and juice from sting nettles. But Mad Etta always joke a lot so we never sure if what she tells us is right. Medicine men never tell their secrets to no-one, that be the first thing Mad Etta teach me when she make me her assistant.

In a week or so Winnie Bear be able to do a couple of things by herself. She still look far away a lot of the time but her eyes that at first look like they been painted on her face with blue paint, sort of get back some of their life.

Etta make her drink lots of things that she cook up for her. All across one wall of her cabin Etta got shelves lined up with different coloured tobacco tins, in some of them are leaves and roots, others got porcupine quills, pig bristles and a whole lots of them have things I don't recognize that smell scary and look worse.

The spring before Winnie get sick we been help Rufus build his cabin up on the hill, cause he figure when Winnie Bear come for the summer she going to stay and live with him, maybe even get married. I sure worry about that some, because the last summer they was here Pauline and Winnie be growed up some and not near so interested in hang around with us guys as they had been. They used to go out to the highway, hitch-hike rides up to Wetaskiwin and run around with white guys there. Guys who got cars and money for beer, cigarettes and Chinese food. Sometimes they don't get home until morning and I can see Rufus ain't very happy, but he figure anyway that if he build that nice cabin Winnie Bear like it so much that she stay with him.

After about a month of doctoring, Winnie Bear start to talk again, and pretty soon she be well enough to do a lot for herself. Soon as she sees Winnie Bear is okay, Pauline she take off for the city. Some people say they seen her around the bars in Edmonton, make lots of parties and mess around mainly with white men.

Rufus build his cabin from logs he cut down himself and it look pretty good. Things like windows and doors and stuff for finish up the inside we get by what we call creative borrowing. That is we borrow Blind Louis Coyote's pick-up truck and cruise around the construction sites up around Wetaskiwin and help ourself to whatever been left lay around.

Etta sure do a good job on that fawn's leg. In a couple of hours it be able to move around some. Etta say we should keep it off its feet for a few days. Somebody get out a baby bottle and the kids come around and take turns feed it milk, especially Winnie Bear. She sit right down on the floor, hold it in her arms and feed it like a baby. Winnie and the kids around the reserve get along real good. She play with them all the time and she laugh a lot, just like she done the first years she was here. The last while she had Rufus make her up a butterfly net and she been out chasing butterflies again.

I guess her being a little girl in her head don't stop her body from having feelings like a woman. At least Rufus say it don't.

After Mad Etta doctor on Winnie for about three months Rufus he be able to move her into his cabin. We have a big party for them, everybody give things for their house and old Red Raven play the fiddle and everybody, even Winnie Bear, is dance around some. She love Rufus a lot, I think, and they seem to get along pretty good, except that Rufus would still like for Mad Etta to make Winnie all the way better, and he say he never gonna stop trying to do that cause he love her so much.

It sure surprise me that after she get Winnie Bear part way fixed up, Etta stop work on her and say she done all she can. Rufus beg her to keep on but she just turn her big buffalo back on him and refuse to speak about it.

I figure that what I gonna do is learn all I can from Mad Etta and then one day I be able to cure Winnie Bear.

This last week or so I been help Rufus and Winnie fix up their cabin some. Mainly Rufus, Winnie try to help but she make mostly a mess. One time she dropped her cheese sandwich in the paint and we all laugh until we cry some and she hug Rufus' neck and tell him she love him a lot because he not get mad at her.

This afternoon Rufus he went down to Hobbema to buy some weatherstrip. Winnie and I be painting the ends of the logs on their cabin when Rufus get home. We paint the little round ends, one red, one yellow, one red again. Winnie laugh a lot and I bet she got more paint on her jeans than on the cabin. Yellow be her favourite colour.

"Mad Etta took the splint off the fawn's leg today," Rufus is say. "That leg was healed up good as new. Boy, that fawn was gone off into the bush in nothing flat. That Mad Etta sure be one good medicine doctor, most of the time."

scars

It is Miss Waits, an old-time teacher from the Residential School, who stir up the trouble because Mary Snakeskin want to register her dead daughter Rebecca when the school start in the fall.

Miss Waits is slim and tiny with a grey face and short grey hair. She always wear black dresses and been teach the Grade Three class for must be 30 years or more.

I remember Ma telling me about the time maybe twenty years ago when Miss Waits be awful sick. It was the middle of winter and the roads was all drifted four feet deep. They have a phone at the Residential School but can't get a doctor out to the reserve.

When everybody figure for sure Miss Waits is dying, one of the young priests come down to Hobbema for Mad Etta. They find her at our cabin and Ma go along with her. Ma say that Mad Etta walk in front of her and the priest and clear the road just like a snowplow. The young priest joke that they should put a blue light on top of Mad Etta and rent her to the county.

When they get to where Miss Waits is, Ma say her face is a kind of bruise-blue colour, and her breath sound like somebody slow-sawing a board. The priests got some candle burning and Etta first cook the blade of her hunting knife in the flame from one of them, then stab the blade right into Miss Waits' throat. While she got the knife in she twist it some to make a hole. She make a lot of mess with blood, Ma say, but in a few minutes Miss Waits be breathing good and some human colour come back to her face. Etta stay with her for two days until the white doctor from Wetaskiwin can get through the roads. When he get there he say he couldn't of done a better job in an operating room in a hospital.

Miss Waits and Mad Etta been friends ever since.

"Don't you remember that your daughter died?" Miss Waits come right out and ask Mary Snakeskin at that school registration.

"Oh, no," Mary say back and smile real bright, "that's not right at all. That was just a very bad dream I had." She look kind of puzzled for a minute before she go on. "Surprise me that you even know about it. I never tell my dreams to nobody."

Well, they say Miss Waits' eyebrows make it right up to her hair line and she call in the Principal, Mr. Gortner, a couple of priests from the Catholic church, and she say if things don't get straighteend around in a hurry she call in the Indian Affairs people, who always hang around on the edge of everything like coyotes look for free food.

But Mary just be polite, smile pretty and say she want to register for school her daughter Rebecca. Her daughter been dead since last year at Indian summer time.

I was there when it happened. Me and my friend Frank Fence-post was ride our horses down the trail from Blue Quills Hall toward Rat Lake. Rat Lake ain't much of a lake:

146

it got muskeg around it on three sides, and a stand of birch and tall grass on the fourth. The Indian summer sun make me sweat and the air smell like it been washed clean. There don't be any flies or mosquitoes or dust, and I can smell the horses and hear the crunch their feet make in the leaves.

When we get near the lake we can hear kids laugh and squeal. I can tell by the sound that some of them be swimming on the other side of the bulrushes, probably my littlest sister Delores and some of her friends. The lake all of a sudden got bigger a few years ago, spilled right over into a stand of poplar trees. The trees is dead now and stand smooth grey against the sky like permanent forked lightning.

When the kids shriek a few crows lift up in the air like they been tossed by a juggler. I'm ride an old horse with hooves must weigh 50 pounds each, but Frank got a horse that dance sideways all the time, and at the sound of the kids it get excited and kick its feet until it get one back one caught in a stirrup. It dance around on three legs. Frank look back and say, "Hey, if you want to get on I'll get off."

About the time we got the horse untangled and calmed down, my sister, Delores and a couple of other little girls come run up from the edge of Rat Lake. Their bodies are about the same colour as the grass and little drops of water sit on their arms and shoulders like beads. Their hair is flat against their heads and none of them going to need the top half of their bathing suits for at least five years.

We is ready to make jokes and tease them some until Delores grab my hand and pull me toward the lake.

"Rebecca's gone," they say.

"When we heard the horses coming we hided under the water," Delores say. "After a while the rest of us come up but Rebecca don't."

"Maybe she's hiding just to scare you?" say Frank.

"No. It's been a long time. We think she drownded."

The girls with Delores are sisters, Jenny and Helen Bottle. Rebecca must be Mary Snakeskin's little girl.

We don't know what to do for sure. We stand and look

out at the lake. It seem to all of a sudden get quieter than it ever been before.

I don't swim, but Frank he get undressed right down to his shorts and go in the water. The girls show him the last place they seen Rebecca and he dive down there a couple of times but can't find anything.

Finally we all head back to town. I got Delores in front of me and Jenny Bottle behind. The other little girl, Helen, ride with Frank. All three girls is crying. We sure hate to leave the lake all alone in case Rebecca turn up but really we know that there ain't no chance.

Soon as we get down to Hobbema we tell around what happen and send Mad Etta over to Mary Snakeskin's cabin to tell her the bad news. Mary make a terrible fuss, scream and yell and call down bad names on everybody.

Mary is about 30, kind of round all over, keep her hair in braids and wear a buckskin skirt and moccasins she make herself. She work at the hockey arena, in the concession booth and sell tickets, and make a real nice home for her and Rebecca. Her husband was a bad dude who went off to rodeo one summer and never come back. Somebody say he down around Gleichen and live with a Peigan girl there.

We all lift a rowboat up on the back of Louis Coyote's pickup truck and we haul it out to Rat Lake. People line up cars along the shore with the lights shine out over the water. It get cold in the night. The air be sharp as broken glass and the moon hang bright as a streetlight above the lake. We ain't got no proper stuff to drag the lake with. RCMP say if we don't find the body in a couple of days they loan us theirs.

On each end of the rowboat we got a torch burn and the light break up on the lake water just like somebody tossed a handful of copper coins. Mad Etta been have to look after Mary Snakeskin and at the same time brew up some medicine. Close to morning we take Etta out on the boat. She sit at the front and about four of us guys sit at the back to balance the weight. The water is lap over the edge of the boat.

"Sure hope you don't gain no weight while we out here," say Frank Fence-post. "We is about one pound away from all of us sinking."

"If this here boat sink, you just hang on to Etta. Etta be big enough she make an island," and she laugh and laugh, make water splash in on my feet. It is a sad laugh even though she try to joke and carry off over the muskeg for miles in the cold air.

Etta take a medicine bag full of stuff she brewed up and float it off from the front of the boat near the spot where the girls last seen Rebecca. The sky glow a little off in the East and the water be the cold colour of a blackboard. We is all tired and cold and quiet. Then there is this awful sound like a boot makes stepping out of the mud, and Rebecca Snakeskin's body float to the surface.

Her mother scream on the shore and it take a couple of guys to hold her from throw herself into the lake.

It seem like an awful thing to say but it would of been better if it was one of the Bottle girls that died. Annie Bottle and about nine kids live poor as coyotes with a mean husband. Rebecca Snakeskin was Mary's only child.

The funeral be a bad scene too and after it for about three weeks Mary Snakeskin don't come out of her cabin. Everybody try to be nice on her but she hardly talk to anybody and when she do she blame them for kill her little girl. "Sad people say a lot more than they mean," say Mad Etta, and shrug her buffalo-big shoulders. "She'll come around."

After a while people go about their own business and leave Mary alone. Everybody got their own troubles.

Nobody paid any attention when it first started, but Jenny Bottle make some calls on Mrs. Snakeskin. I don't know why she done it, maybe just because she have a good heart. Jenny is I guess eight years old, skinny, with a pinched face, but tough as red willow. Her eyes is close together and her skin tight on her bones, not the least bit like Rebecca, who was short and round like her mama.

Jenny begin to spend a lot of time with Mary Snakeskin and everybody who see what is happening say that it is a good thing. She stay overnight at Mary's cabin and walk down to Hobbema General Store to buy groceries for her. When the hockey season get going strong Mary go back to her job. Everybody is some happy for her. It is only then, though, that people learn about the funny way she see the world. She all the time talk to the other ladies at the concession stand about her little girl Rebecca as though she was alive, and one night when Jenny Bottle come to see her at work, Mary call her Rebecca, and talk to Jenny like she was her dead daughter.

Pretty soon Jenny start to live in with Mary full time. Jenny start to grow a little meat on her bones and Mary buy her some warm clothes for the winter like she never had before.

Etta always like to keep a jump or two ahead of any trouble on the reserve so she take me along over to Annie Bottle's place one summer afternoon. Fred Bottle is off in jail for a month or so, so this be one of the better times for Annie. Her cabin smell of grease and mouldy things, and there be a whole bunch of kids sit around on a mattress that lay in the corner on the floor.

Annie wear a long skirt of a purple colour with lots of stains on it, and a kerchief tied tight over her head and knotted under her chin. She walk like an old woman and all the time look at the ground.

Etta talk about small things, look at a couple of the kids that Annie say been sick, and say she'll bring over some stuff to cure their ringworm.

"So what do you hear from Jenny?" she finally say.

Annie mumble something in Cree that I can't make out. She raise up her eyes that are tiny and dull. "I'm glad she got a better place," she say.

Annie got a bad scar all the way from her ear to the corner of her nose on the left side. I hear tell that Fred Bottle bust a plate on her face one time when he was drunk. Annie look like people been beating on her all her life. Seeing Annie Bottle live the way she do is the reason I believe in a heaven of some kind. There got to be a better place than

Hobbema for people like Annie after they die.

"I'm glad she got a better place," is the only words Annie speak of her daughter.

On the way back Etta say, "So who's it doing any harm to? Little Rebecca's dead, but if Mary want to get a new kid to take her place, and call *her* Rebecca, then what's the harm?"

"Hey, I'm your assistant, remember? You don't have to convince me. It white peoples who think that what's going on is funny."

"Most everything in the world is funny if you look at it from the right angle," say Etta. Seem to me everybody be getting along okay and they stay that way unless white peoples come along to mess it up.

Etta, I guess, know that it just be a matter of time. It be just a month or so later that Mary Snakeskin try to register Jenny in the Grade Three class.

Mary pretend that Miss Waits don't bother her none. Guess maybe it ain't pretend. Mary's face is clear and round, so smooth and shiny it could be waxed like the hardwood floor at Blue Quills Hall.

Her and Jenny go everywhere together. It is pretty easy to tell by the look on her face that what Mary see when she look at Jenny Bottle is not the frail-shouldered little girl in front of her, but her own dead daughter who liked to dance in front of people and had a laugh bright as sunlight on water.

What we like to do is keep Indian Affairs Department far away from this whole scene. Wouldn't matter a bit to them if Mary and Jenny was happy or not. What they worry about is all the rules they got written down in black books in their offices. Indians might as well be cords of stove wood the way that the Government figure.

Talk around the reserve is that if Indian Affairs get involved they take Jenny away from Mary Snakeskin, get a judge to say that Jenny have to go in a home for kids some place away from the reserve, and maybe Mary have to go in the place for crazy people down at Ponoka.

"I think it about time we walk up there to the school and talk with Miss Waits," say Etta. It got to be a mile or more up to the school and what Etta mean by walk is from her cabin to Blind Louis Coyote's pickup truck which she expect me to borrow and also get some friends to help load and unload her. I get the truck and my friends Frank Fence-post and Rufus Firstrider, put her chair up in the back, then one pull while two of us push Mad Etta up the door from One-wound's outhouse which is what we always go to use for a ramp.

"What do you figure makes Mary the way she is?" I ask.

"Grief have different effect on different people," Etta say. "Some people show their scars, some cover them up and on some people scars don't take."

"I remember once after a thunderstorm," I say, "me and Illianna and Joseph, we went outside and picked up damp rose petals. We stuck them to our faces and they dried there. Look like scars." But it don't seem to me that Etta is listening.

"If you was medicine man, Silas, how would you handle this?" Etta say to me as we tramp up the long path to the teachers' apartment block of the Residential School.

"I tell the truth. I tell Miss Waits how what happen makes Mary a happy person again and how Jenny got a better home than she ever have before, and how it is a kind of make-believe that hurt no-one."

"How do you think that go over with Miss Waits?"

"White peoples don't take no stock in make-believe. They'd have to fill out Government forms before they could have a vision."

"Then what?"

"Maybe you could threaten to cast some bad medicine on her?" Etta shake her head. "We could get Frank to dress up with war paint and a mask and scare her." Even I know that ain't much of an idea. Etta shake her big buffalo head again. "Why do you always got to be smarter than me?" I say. "So what is it you gonna do?"

"When nothing else work," say Etta, "you call in old

debts."

Miss Waits cook up some tea for us.

"Highly irregular," is how Miss Waits describe the situation.

"Would it really hurt your records so much?" say Etta. "Them girls was almost the same age." Then she explain how Jenny got it better than she ever had in her life, and how Mary's pretending don't hurt no-one.

"Highly irregular," Miss Waits say again.

"You let Indian Affairs in on this yet?"

"No," say Miss Waits, and Etta make a sigh that just about blow over some of the little glass animals on the coffee table. Etta don't argue no more and it seem like she given up. They have tea and get to talk about Miss Waits' health.

"Remember the time I knifed you?" Etta say. "I'd of got 90 days in the hoosgow if I'd of done it at the Alice Hotel," and she laugh and laugh.

Miss Waits put her hand to her throat what be covered by a high-necked white blouse. "You saved my life, Etta."

"Kind of give you a second chance."

"Yes."

"Was figuring maybe you wouldn't mind seeing some-body else get a second chance. Even though you don't understand the why of it, maybe you could just sort of trust an old friend." Etta smile at her, but it is a serious smile as she pile about five spoons of sugar in her tea.

"Do you really believe that things are best left alone?" say Miss Waits looking Etta right in the eye but still touch her neck.

Etta nod her huge head up and down.

"You know there's not much I can do now, after all the wheels have been started in motion. There are other people involved . . ." her voice trail off for a minute. She finger her neck again and smile kind of sad. "Of course, I am getting old. I suppose I could have made a mistake . . ."

"If you was to fill out the right forms."

"You know as well as I do, Etta, that those little Indian

girls all look alike." Miss Waits take the teapot which is all wrapped up in a bright blanket like a baby in a crib and fill our cups up again. It look to me like from here on it going to be mostly downhill.

MOUSE HOUSE

MOUSE HOUSE

BY RUMER GODDEN

Illustrated by Adrienne Adams

THE VIKING PRESS · NEW YORK

Fic 1. Mice—Stories

7 8 9 10 11 76 75 74 73 72

PRINTED IN THE U.S.A. BY AFFILIATED LITHOGRAPHERS

For

MARY GROVES,

because Mouse House belonged to her

Once upon a time there was a little mouse house. It was like a doll's house, but not for dolls, for mice.

Its walls were painted red, with lines for bricks. Its roof was gray, with painted tiles and a red chimney. The roof lifted up, and in the

house was a hall with a front door, a sitting room, and a bedroom, each with a window.

The wallpaper had a pattern of spots as small as pinheads, and the carpets were pink flannel. In the hall was a doormat cut from two inches of tweed. The sitting room had a painted fireplace, two chairs, and a table. In the bedroom was a tiny looking glass and a bed with bedclothes and a blue and white quilt. At the window were muslin curtains, and

on each sill stood thimble-sized pots of geraniums; the geraniums were made of scarlet
silk. On tin-tack pegs on the wall hung some
dusters no bigger than postage stamps.

Over the front door was a notice that said,
"MOUSE HOUSE."

Mouse House was given to a girl called
Mary as an Easter present. "It's to keep your
jewelry in," said her father, but Mary shook her
head.

"It's meant for mice," said Mary, and indeed
there were two mice there already, a he-mouse
in the sitting room and a she-mouse in the bedroom. They wore clothes; He-mouse had a suit
with a pale blue ribbon tie; She-mouse wore a
dress with a pale blue apron. They stood on their
hind legs, and their fur looked just like flannel,

their whiskers looked like bristles, and their eyes were as still as beads.

"Are you proper mice?" asked Mary. There was no answer, not so much as a squeak.

He-mouse and She-mouse stayed quite still, quite, quite still.

Mary was disappointed. "I thought mice ran," she said.

Most mice do. They scamper up and down the stairs and come into the larder and the cupboards and climb the table legs. They whisk into holes and run behind the wainscoting. The sound of their running can make a rustle and patter like rain, and they go so fast you can hardly believe you have seen them. That is how most mice run, but not He-mouse and She-mouse.

Mary waited for them to move—"Even a tail or a whisker," said Mary. Sometimes she lifted the roof up quietly to take a sudden peep, but they were always standing where she had left them; still, quite, quite still.

At last she took Mouse House upstairs and put it away on her chest-of-drawers.

"Don't you want to play with it?" asked her mother.

"Mice can't play," said Mary, but she was wrong.

Far down, below-stairs, in Mary's house, was a cellar where rubbish was kept, and there, behind an old broom in the corner, was another mouse house. It was not elegant like the one upstairs. It was a broken flowerpot made comfortable with hay. I cannot tell you how many mice lived in it because I was never quick enough to catch them, but it was brimful of mice.

"This overcrowding in houses is a terrible problem," Mary's father said as he read the newspaper. The mice in the flowerpot could have told him that.

When they were all in it asleep there were always some whiskers or a tail hanging out, an ear, a paw, or a little mouse leg. There was not an eighth of an an inch to spare—if you want to know how small that is, look on a school ruler—and the youngest, a little girl mouse called Bonnie, ended up most nights pushed out on the cellar floor.

"She will catch cold," said Mother Mouse. "It's bad to lie out on the stone."

Father Mouse scolded the children. "Naughty!
Bad mice!" he said.

"They can't help it," said Mother Mouse.
"There are too many of them."

Then he scolded her. "You shouldn't have had
so many," he said.

But they were beautiful children. Their fur
was soft and brown, not at all like flannel; their
ears and tails were apple-blossom pink; and their

whiskers were fine, not like bristles. Their eyes
were black and busy, not still, like beads, and all
day those mouse children darted and scampered

and played. Mary would not have believed her
eyes if she had seen them. Even when they were
asleep they scrabbled and twitched as if they
were running in their dreams. "But I wish they
wouldn't," said Bonnie.

"Couldn't we move to a larger house?" she

asked. "Couldn't we find one? Couldn't we *look?*"
asked Bonnie. But there was no time; with such
a big family to feed, Father and Mother Mouse
were gathering crumbs and bits of cheese and
scraps of this and that from morning to night.

"A-t-*choo!*" sneezed Bonnie.

What games did the mice children play? Much the same as you: catch-as-catch-can and puss-in-the-corner—though puss was really frightening to them. They played I'm-on-Tom-Cat's-Ground-Picking-up-Gold-and-Silver, and blind-mouse-buff and hide-and-seek. Mary would have been surprised. An empty matchbox made them a cart, and for balls they had some dried peas.

"Come and play, Bonnie!" cried her brothers and sisters, but Bonnie had caught a cold and did not want to play. Two tears as small as dew-drops ran down her whiskers; mice do not have handkerchiefs, so that she could not wipe them away.

That night she found herself out on the floor again. "Mammy! Mammy!" squeaked Bonnie, but Mother Mouse was asleep, worn out with searching for crumbs and cheese.

"Mammy! Mammy!"

The cellar was cold and dark. From inside the flowerpot came soft snufflings and squealings, the sound of little mice happily asleep. Bonnie tried to get back, but she could not push in more than the tip of her nose.

"Where can I go?" squeaked Bonnie.

She wrapped herself round in her tail and curled up on the cellar floor, but it was too cold to sleep. She tried once more to push back into the flowerpot, but one of her brothers, dreaming of the cat, kicked her hard in the eye with his paw. "Ouch!" squeaked Bonnie, but no mouse heard.

"Nobody wants me," said poor Bonnie and began to creep away. "Where can I go?" she asked; there was no mouse to tell her. ·

She crept across the cellar floor until she came to a flight of steps. "Shall I go up them?" asked Bonnie. There seemed nowhere else to go.

At the top she rubbed her whiskers; she thought a strange light was shining. "Is it?" asked Bonnie, straining her whiskers to look.

The light was shining at the end of a long passage; it came from under the crack of a door.

A mouse can wriggle under a crack. Bonnie crept down the passage and under the crack and found herself in the hall.

The hall was filled with clear silver light. Bonnie blinked. She had not seen moonlight before. It was very pretty but very strange. It

turned her into a silver mouse, and that made
her feel dizzy.

She crept out on the rug. She had never been
here before—only behind the wainscot—and her
whiskers trembled as she looked this way and
that.

The grandfather clock in the corner went TOCK-TOCK-TOCK-TOCK, and Bonnie's heart, which was not much bigger than a watch, went *tick-tick-tick-tick-tick-tick*, far more quickly. Then it almost stopped.

The cat was asleep on a chair.

Bonnie had only heard about the cat; she had

never seen him; but she knew at once what he was.

W-H-I-S-K! I wish I could describe to you how quickly she was gone up the stairs.

Oh, how her legs ached and her breath hurt! It was like climbing a mountain far too fast.

"He's coming! He's coming!" squeaked Bonnie.

The cat had not moved an eyelid, but Bonnie
was half dead with fright when she reached the
top landing. "A hole! I need a hole!" she
squeaked, but there was no time to look for one,
and she wriggled under the crack of the nearest
door—it was the door of Mary's room.

"I need somewhere high and safe. Another
mountain!" And Bonnie ran up the highest
thing she could see—it was the chest-of-drawers.

"Oh, my poor heart!" cried Bonnie; it was going *tick-tick-tick-tick-tick, tick-tick-tick-tick-
tick* faster than you can say it. Then, there in
front of her, she saw Mouse House.

"It's a hole! It's a house!" cried Bonnie.

The front door was open, and she flicked
inside.

For a long time she lay in the hall. Then, when
she was sure she was really safe, she sniffed the
doormat with her whiskers.

She looked into the sitting room. He-mouse
was there.

"Hello," said Bonnie.

There was no answer.

She touched He-mouse with her whiskers—
which is the mouse way of shaking hands—but
he did not touch her back.

"It looks like a mouse, but it does not feel like
a mouse nor smell like a mouse," said Bonnie.

She went into the bedroom. She-mouse was
there.

"Hello," said Bonnie.

There was no answer.

Bonnie touched She-mouse with her whiskers,
but She-mouse did not touch her back.

"It looks like a mouse, but it does not feel like
a mouse nor smell like a mouse," said Bonnie.

"Can't you hear me?" Bonnie asked.

She-mouse did not say "Yes," and she did not say "No"; she said nothing at all.

"Pay attention," said Bonnie and flipped She-mouse with her tail.

She-mouse fell flat on her back on the floor.

Bonnie went back into the sitting room, where He-mouse had not moved.

"You had better lie down too," said Bonnie and flipped *him* with her tail.

He-mouse fell flat on his back on the floor.

That made Bonnie remember how much she wanted to lie down herself, not stiff and straight as they did, but curled up soft and warm. "Aaaahh!" She gave a yawn.

She tried to lie on the chairs, but they were too small. The table was too hard. She went into the bedroom and looked at herself in the glass, and the mouse in the glass gave a yawn too. "Poor little mouse. How sleepy you are!" said Bonnie. Then she turned and saw the bed.

She had not seen a bed before, but she knew at once what it was for. Whisk! Up she jumped and wriggled under the quilt. It is true that she put her tail on the pillow, but a very young mouse cannot be expected to know everything.

The bed was soft, the quilt was warm; in a minute Bonnie was fast asleep.

She was so tired that she slept a long, long
time. When she woke up in the morning, someone had shut the front door.

Have you ever been shut in? Then you will
know how it feels. Bonnie ran round from room
to room, round and round and round. She pressed
her face against the windows until her whiskers
hurt; she bruised her paws in beating on the
door.

The table and chairs, the bed and the geraniums, were all knocked over; the looking glass
came off the wall and the dusters were twitched

off their pegs. The wallpaper was scratched off and the carpets were torn.

"Let me out! Let me out!" squeaked Bonnie, but nobody heard. There was no one to hear. Mary had gone down to breakfast.

He-mouse and She-mouse lay flat on the floor; Bonnie ran over and over them, but they did not protest.

"Mammy! Mammy!" squeaked Bonnie. "I want to go home."

Far down below in the cellar Mother Mouse was squeaking.

"Be quiet and let me sleep," said Father Mouse, but she would not let him sleep.

"A mouse child is missing," she squeaked, and she shook him. "A mouse child is missing, is missing!"

"How do you know?" asked Father Mouse, and he tumbled slowly out of bed. He slept in the bottom of the flowerpot and got up last of all.

"I counted them," said Mother Mouse.

"*You* can't count," said Father Mouse. Neither

could he, but he did not tell her that. He watched
the mice children hopping and skipping about.
"They are all here," he said.

But Mother Mouse shook her whiskers. "There
should be one more." She pulled all the hay out
of the flowerpot; there were some bits of cheese
rind, but no mouse child was there. She wept,
but Father Mouse quickly ate up the cheese rind.
It was his private store.

Upstairs in Mouse House Bonnie ran round
and round.

When the flowerpot was empty, how dirty and small it looked. "How can anyone be expected to bring up children in *that?*" said Mother Mouse.

"What's the matter with it?" asked Father.

"It's dirty and shabby and broken and small," said Mother Mouse. "There's a hole in the bottom—a little mouse could fall straight through it or be cut on the jagged edges or fall out on the cellar floor. You must find me another house at once!" said Mother Mouse.

"What, *me?*" said Father Mouse. "I'm eating." And I am sorry to say that with his mouth full he said, "The houth ith for the children. Leth the children look."

The mouse children were delighted. "A new house? We'll find one!" they cried and ran squeaking all over the cellar floor.

They found an old coal scuttle, but it was full of soot. "We should be black mice," said Mother Mouse.

They found a flour bin with a hole in it, but all

the flour had not run out. "We should be white mice," said Mother Mouse.

A riding boot looked cosy, but: "What a long long passage," said Mother Mouse. "And it's dark. It needs a window at the other end."

There was no more room in a kettle than in the flowerpot, and a dustpan was not the right shape.

"It's too difficult to find a house," said the
mouse children. They lay down in the hay and
went to sleep. Father Mouse slept too, but
Mother Mouse sat up. She wanted a new house
and she was missing her baby. Every now and
again a mouse tear slid to the end of her
whiskers.

And upstairs in Mouse House poor Bonnie ran
round and round. "Let me out! Let me out!" she
squeaked.

Every morning after breakfast Mary made her bed. This morning, when she came into the room, she heard a queer noise; it was rustlings and scratchings and thumps and squeaks. It seemed to come from Mouse House. Mary listened: squeaks and thumps and scratchings and rustlings, and it did come from Mouse House! "My mice are *playing!*" cried Mary.

She ran to lift up the roof and look . . . and nearly dropped it.

Quick as a flash, with a flip and a thud, Bonnie had jumped out. WHISK! She ran down the chest-of-drawers and out through the bedroom door. All Mary saw was a flash of whisker and tail.

"They've gone!" cried Mary, but when she turned over the mess in Mouse House, He-mouse and She-mouse were flat on the floor.

"Then was there *another* mouse?" asked Mary.

What a sight Mouse House was now! The curtains were down, the paper was in ribbons, and

the carpets were ripped. Chairs and bedclothes,
geraniums and dusters were all mixed up; the
legs had come off the table; the quilt was torn
to bits. "It's all spoiled," said Mary.

There was nothing to do with Mouse House
but to put it down in the cellar.

Bonnie took a long time to reach home. She ran into a hole in the wainscot on the landing and lost her way. All day she trotted up and down those wainscot passages. Once she came out into the hall and met the cat; then she got into the bathroom where a lady was washing in the basin. "A mouse! A mouse!" screamed the lady and threw a sponge. The sponge landed on the floor by Bonnie and made her soaking wet.

It was not until late that evening that a tired, cold, dirty, draggled little mouse put her whiskers out of another hole and found she was in the cellar. She was just going to run to the flowerpot, when what did she see?

She shook her whiskers once, twice, three
times before she could believe her eyes. The
flowerpot was gone, and where it had stood,
under the old broom, was Mouse House.

But what a different Mouse House! It was full
of scufflings and squeakings; out of every window and even up the chimney peeped little mice.

Father Mouse was in the hall, and on the door-step Mother Mouse was looking anxiously this way and that.

"Mammy! Mammy!" squeaked Bonnie.

"I *knew* there was one more!" said Mother Mouse.

For the mice, Mouse House was not spoiled at
all; they found it far more convenient without
curtains and a table and chairs.

They used one room for sleeping in, the other
as a pantry. "That's better," said Mother Mouse.
"It *is* better not to have cheese rind in the beds."

Father Mouse hid a little under the doormat in
the hall.

The scraps of wallpaper and carpet and bedclothes made a comfortable nest; the girl mice
wrapped each of the geraniums in a duster and
used them for dolls.

What happened to He-mouse and She-mouse? Mary had lifted them out of the house at once but they did not seem to notice when it was taken away, or that He-mouse's tie was off and

She-mouse's apron torn. "And it wasn't *you* playing," said Mary.

She tidied them up and sewed them on a pin-cushion and gave it to her aunt for Christmas.

The mice are very happy, particularly Bonnie.
She was a little nervous at first of being shut
into Mouse House, but the door soon came off its
hinges, with the mouse traffic going in and out.
When her brothers and sisters heard her story
they voted she should sleep in the bed. "So that
she can never be pushed out again," said Mother
Mouse.

"But if I hadn't been pushed out," said wise
little Bonnie, "we shouldn't have Mouse House."

[61]

How do I know all this? Well, one day, not a
long time after, Mary hid in the cellar when *she*
played hide-and-seek. As she sat there, quite
quiet, the mice children came hopping out;
hopping and skipping and scampering and
jumping. "Then mice *do* play," said Mary.

After that she would often steal down to
watch and listen and look.

"They are *my* mice," said Mary. "I gave them Mouse House."

Then she stopped and thought, Or did one little mouse come and fetch it?

When she had thought that, I think she could guess the rest, and that is how she came to tell me, and I to tell you, the story of Mouse House.